Explorers
Thoughts on Mapping in Design Research

Edited by Megan Anderson & Geke van Dijk / STBY

with contributions from Stephen Bennet, Brian Blankinship, Sanne van den Breemer, Constance Chung, Cat Drew, Dorota Gazy, Jesse Grimes, Michael Johnson, Chris Marmo, Kate McLean, Sophie Knight, Bas Raijmakers, Katharina Rainer, Michael Steingress, Marc Stickdorn, Daphne Stylianou, Shay Raviv, and Zeynep Yavuz.

Explorers: Thoughts on Mapping in Design Research

Editors: Megan Anderson and Geke van Dijk (STBY)

Contributors: Marc Stickdorn and Katharina Rainer (Smaply), Jesse Grimes, Bas Raijmakers (STBY), Sophie Knight, Michael Johnson (Glasgow School of Art), Cat Drew (Design Council), Sanne van den Breemer (The Berlage), Brian Blankinship (Omplexity), Michael Steingras (More than Metrics), Constance Chung, Daphne Stylianou (STBY), Dorota Gazy (STBY), Kate McLean, Zeynep Yavuz (CLEVER°FRANKE), Shay Raviv, Stephen Bennet (Policy Lab).

Graphic design: Hyperkit

Printer: Swallowtail

Edition: 1000

Publisher:
STBY Ltd.
De Beauvoir Block, unit 5
92-96 De Beauvoir Road
London N1 4EN
United Kingdom
www.stby.eu
info@stby.eu

ISBN: 978-1-5272-7182-1

..STBY...

Preface

Robert Louis Stevenson, author of *Treasure Island*, once said, "I am told there are people who do not care for maps, and I find it hard to believe." This is particularly relevant among designers and researchers, who all love a good map. Stakeholder maps, ecosystem maps, service blueprints, customer journey maps, and the like have become common tools of our trade. We use maps for all sorts of things, from mapping knowledge gaps at the beginning of a project to communicating research findings at the end. We use maps to discover, collaborate, plan, brainstorm, and tell stories. We use maps to get lost and find our way again.

The formats and processes for mapping in our field have largely emerged from practice, much like a craft. While maps have become tacit artifacts, the process of mapping remains mysterious in many ways. Increasingly, as practitioners deal with more systemic issues, we are beginning to see the need for more refined tools and language with which to address such complexity and uncertainty. We need to get better at talking and thinking about mapping as a collaborative sense-making activity.

The process of mapping is just as important as the map itself. Ultimately mapping is hard work that needs to embrace uncertainty and explore unknowns. The rich history of mapping tells us to keep questioning maps, and to avoid falling into the trap of thinking that a map can ever be completely accurate. From which perspective do you map? Can you integrate multiple perspectives? How much detail do you provide and how do you choose what to omit? Such moments of doubt and uncertainty are very important in the process towards a 'final' map and require a lot of research and analysis, in addition to many tough decisions.

Luckily, designers and researchers aren't the only people who do a lot of mapping. Systems visualisation is something practiced across disciplines and there is a lot we can learn and adapt from various fields. Concepts like projection, selection, generalisation, and deconstruction from cartography are all quite relevant to our process, for example. The process of drafting from architecture and engineering helps articulate the iterative process of moving from abstract visualisation toward more precision. And the idea of nested systems from systems science helps us understand and conceptualise how systems are embedded in, and interconnected with, one another. The list goes on.

Looking further afield not only helps us adopt useful frames for our own processes; it helps us to define and articulate what is unique and distinct when it comes to mapping in our own practice. We hope this collection of thoughts and maps will spark conversations and debate, and help us all move forward more confidently into uncharted territory.

Illustration by Harry Furniss in *Sylvie and Bruno Concluded*

"What a useful thing a pocket-map is!" I remarked.

"That's another thing we've learned from your Nation," said Mein Herr, "map-making. But we've carried it much further than you. What do you consider the largest map that would be really useful?"

"About six inches to the mile."

"Only six inches!" exclaimed Mein Herr. "We very soon got to six yards to the mile. Then we tried a hundred yards to the mile. And then came the grandest idea of all ! We actually made a map of the country, on the scale of a mile to the mile!"

"Have you used it much?" I enquired.

"It has never been spread out, yet," said Mein Herr: "the farmers objected: they said it would cover the whole country, and shut out the sunlight! So we now use the country itself, as its own map, and I assure you it does nearly as well."

from *Lewis Carroll, Sylvie and Bruno Concluded*, Chapter XI, London, 1895

Contents

New Territories

About STBY

STBY is a design research consultancy specialised in design research for service innovation. Based in London and Amsterdam, our creative research projects connect organisations with the lives and experiences of their customers. This helps our clients in industry and the public sector to innovate their service offering, adding value to both their customers and the organisation. Our projects generate rich, visually illustrated and engaging materials, that bring real people into the heart of service innovation processes.

As a pioneer in the field of design research and service design, STBY is always keen on experimenting, learning, and knowledge exchange with peers. This publication is the result of such a self-initiated R&D project. Previous publications in this series were VIEWFINDERS and PIONEERS. More info on www.stby.eu

As always, the full STBY has been involved in the production of this publication. Apart from writing and copy editing, this also entails layout, references and image credits. Special thanks to Esther van Roosmalen, Nina Stegeman, Qin Han, Yoni Lefévre and Fanechka Fernandes.

About the editors

Megan Anderson

Megan is a Design Researcher at STBY London. She has experience working with a range of public and private sector clients including Spotify, Google, HM Treasury and The London Fire Brigade. She is also a lead researcher for the What Design Can Do Challenges.

Previously, Megan conducted graduate research at Leiden University, with a focus on collaboration and innovation in the public safety sector. She has published on the topics of public safety policy, design research and game-inspired collaborative planning. She is also a map-obsessed trail runner, aspiring spy fiction podcaster, and proud RSA fellow. Originally from Singapore, Megan has lived and worked in Taiwan, Australia, The Netherlands and The United Kingdom.

Geke van Dijk

Geke is co-founder and Strategy Director of STBY. She has a background in ethnographic research, user-centered design and service strategy. Her passion to bring people into the heart and soul innovation processes, and her strong drive to contribute to positive change in society has shaped the direction of STBY's portfolio of working on topics such as community participation, inclusivity and sustainability.

Since founding STBY in 2003, Geke has been one of the early pioneers in the field of Service Design. She was the initiator of the Service Design Network Netherlands, and has been their chair for 10 years. She is also a co-founder of the REACH Network for Global Design Research. Geke frequently publishes presents and teaches on Service Innovation and Design Research. She holds a PhD in Computer Sciences from the Open University in the UK.

About the contributors

This publication has been made possible by generous contributions from a wonderful network of mapping innovators working in various fields. A big thank you to: Marc Stickdorn and Katharina Rainer (More than Metrics), Jesse Grimes, Bas Raijmakers (STBY), Sophie Knight, Michael Johnson (Glasgow School of Art), Cat Drew (Design Council), Sanne van den Breemer (The Berlage), Brian Blankinship (Omplexity), Michael Steingras (More than Metrics), Constance Chung, Daphne Stylianou (STBY), Dorota Gazy (STBY), Kate McLean, Zeynep Yavuz (CLEVER°FRANKE), Shay Raviv, Stephen Bennet (Policy Lab).

Brief biographies for each contributor can be found at the bottom of their article.

Image credits for the visuals in the article are listed at the end of the publication (page 95-96).

You Are Here

Beyond journey maps and personas

State of the art in system mapping for service design

By Katharina Rainer and Marc Stickdorn (More than Metrics)

Since the rise of service design, system maps have been attracting increasing interest. A growing number of people are becoming aware of the insights you can derive from the combination of system maps alongside journey maps and personas.

For over a decade, system maps have been at the heart of our activities at More than Metrics. Since co-authoring the book *This is Service Design Thinking*[1] in 2010, we have been observing the development of system maps closely. Later, when we launched Smaply[2] in 2012, one of the pioneering tools we offered was system mapping in the form of a digital, online stakeholder map. Hence, we have had the chance to observe how people started using this tool more and more, and how they increasingly involved larger teams in their system mapping activities.

Looking back at our logfiles since 2012, it is clear that system maps did not get as much attention as they do now. Year after year we have observed how the interest in system maps has increased. This is also reflected in the direct feedback we get from our users and partners, and the numbers of people attending our training sessions or seeking detailed information.

A system map of an airport experience from a Smaply demo project.

Understanding the 'jungle' of stakeholders and relationships

The term 'system map' in service design is an umbrella term for stakeholder maps (which players are involved?), value network maps (how are players connected?), and ecosystem maps (what technologies, products, systems, stakeholders, and other entities are involved?). For those who are rather new to system mapping, you can find an introduction to the different types of system maps in the method library[3] of This is Service Design Doing (TISDD).

System maps are a great tool to clarify and understand the 'jungle' of stakeholders involved in a project, and at the same time the relationships between them. System maps offer a versatile tool that can be used at different stages of a service design project, from understanding existing

stakeholder networks to designing new networks based on the context and perspective of a specific project.

System maps are an essential part of holistic service design projects. They are often closely connected to other essential tools, such as personas and customer journeys. System maps help to analyse and clarify what most influences the key experiences of specific personas at various steps of a customer journey. In this way, system maps significantly contribute to the big picture with a detailed analysis of each service element.

Not so long ago, system maps were only perceived as a nice add-on to customer journey maps. But now we clearly see an increasing number of users of Smaply searching for and actively using our dedicated system mapping tool as part of their core activities.

Applying and scaling system mapping in organisations

For many of our more experienced enterprise customers we see that system maps have become a crucial part of their work. Many of them are already familiar with journey maps and personas, but are looking to finally get a bigger picture of their service and to see their customers, employees and other stakeholders in their wider context. We get more and more requests for the use of our system mapping tool, as well as for team training sessions on how to best apply and scale it.

We had the chance to draft best practice reports with some of our customers. Here, we introduce two of them, both conducted in industries that are rather new to service design, but developing fast: healthcare and human resources.

System mapping in healthcare

The first example is a project conducted with Community Empowerment Lab (CEL), a global health research and innovation organisation based in India. They used stakeholder maps to better understand and redesign the context of newborns and their mothers in rural India.

Stakeholder maps helped project teams widen their perspective on who is involved in their service. Often they are not aware of the crucial roles that less visible stakeholders play. Stakeholder mapping helped the project team understand the crucial work of nurses throughout the process. Hence, they used system maps to better understand the context of these nurses and make them

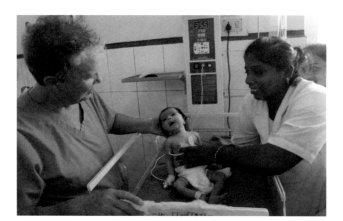

Above: Dr. Barbara Morission (left) advising the staff nurses at Raebareli district women's hospital Uttar Pradesh.

Below: In the stakeholder map the team could see that many of the stakeholders were connected with each other, directly and indirectly. The stakeholder map was useful when looking at a micro environment, e.g. a mother in a KMC lounge and the people who influence her in that environment.

Opposite right: A nurse's journey map (exported from Smaply).

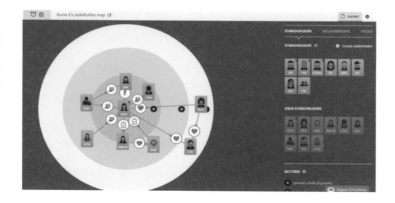

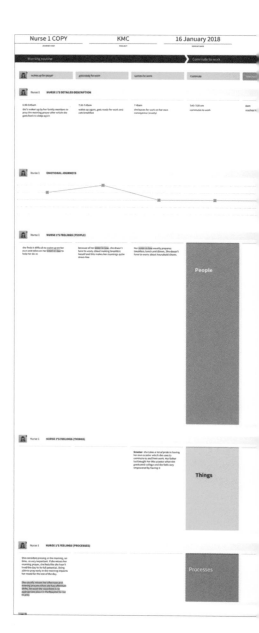

an essential part of the redesign of the service. They used system maps to look at a micro environment, e.g. how a mother is influenced by the people in an environment.

Read the full case study[4] on the Smaply blog.

System mapping in human resources

The second example is a project in collaboration with hkkp// group, an international consulting company specialized in HR topics such as performance management, talent management and compensation. They organised a series of events for BPM, the German Federal Association of HR Managers, to introduce HR managers to customer experience management.

Participants from across Germany, and of diverse company sizes and industries, learned how to apply service design methods to HR to boost their employee

experience and increase employee loyalty towards the company. They used stakeholder maps to better understand how work connects to the private life of employees. They specifically focused on the three topics of career development and further education, recognition and work-life balance.

Read the full case study[5] on the Smaply blog.

State of the art use of system maps

System maps can be used for a wide range of purposes. The most classic use case is to make it a central part of the kick off session of a service design project, to understand what parties are involved in a service from a customer or persona point-of-view. This helps to find useful interview partners and identify who needs to be considered when optimizing the experience. At that moment, system maps

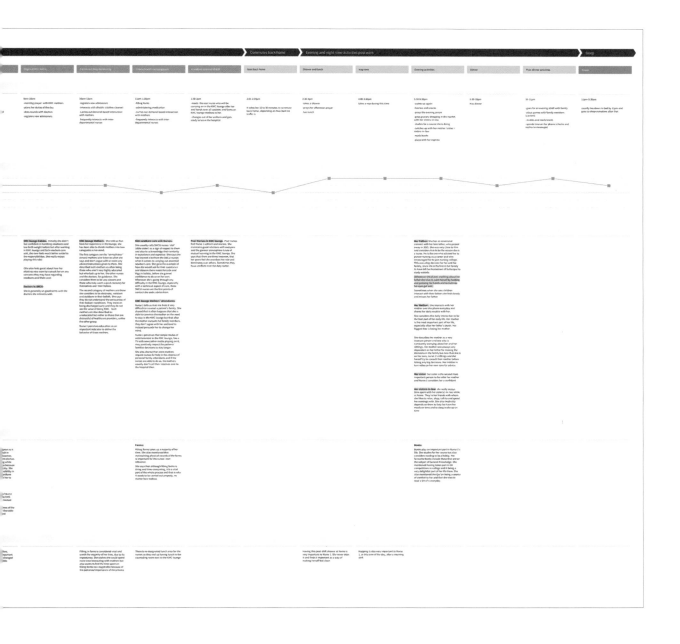

are still mostly assumption-based. Over time and over the course of the project, more data is then collected and the assumption-based system map gradually turns into a research-based system map that enables further decision-making.

System maps are traditionally used to improve customer experiences by putting the customer at the center of the analysis. And lately, since employee experiences are gaining more attention from companies, system maps are also increasingly used in that context. Just put an employee in the centre of the system map and arrange important stakeholders around the map according to their importance to the employee.

Another interesting use of system maps is to better understand an organisation itself. Which internal or external stakeholders are involved in the organisation's key processes? Or in the case of a particular project, who should become part of the project team? Who needs to be informed and how? Which decision makers need to be convinced?

After the development of a current-state system map, it can be used to draft a future-state system map. From here it can be used to test different scenarios: which relationships are missing? Which elements need to be removed, added or strengthened?

At this point you can begin to see possibilities for strengthening certain relationships or touch points, or add completely new ones altogether. For example, you may uncover that a specific relationship has been neglected even though there is high potential for valuable business. This leads to a final big strength: through system mapping it becomes possible to reveal blindspots and uncover new business opportunities.

Katharina Rainer is Head of Marketing and Communications at More than Metrics. She has a Master of Science in Strategic Management from The University of Innsbruck.

Marc Stickdorn is the cCo-founder and CEO of More than Metrics. He is also a visiting / adjunct professor at various business and design schools. In 2010, Marc and Jakob Schneider published the award-winning book *This is Service Design Thinking*.

More than Metrics develops service design and customer journey mapping tools, like Smaply, for companies that want to improve their customer experience. Smaply is a web-based software that illustrates journey maps, personas, and stakeholder maps.

1 http://www.tisdt.com

2 https://www.smaply.com

3 https://www.thisisservicedesigndoing.com/methods

4 https://www.smaply.com/blog/case-study-health-care

5 https://www.smaply.com/blog/service-design-hr

Case study

Mapping the death of a loved one to improve government services

The Digital Transformation Agency asked us to conduct research that asked Australians — 'What's it like to deal with the death of someone close to you?'

By Chris Marmo (Paper Giant)

Researching death in Australia
Coping with the death of a loved one is one of the most difficult events in anyone's life. Although death affects us all at some point, Australians rarely prepare for it, and the topic itself is still taboo.

Over 10 weeks, we conducted in-depth interviews with over 40 people who had recently experienced the death of a loved one. This research required a carefully considered ethical approach to research, in which care for our participants and staff was paramount.

We collected a diverse range of experiences from people of different ages, socioeconomic backgrounds, geographic locations, and cultural and linguistic communities, including Aboriginal Australians. We also spoke to service providers, including medical staff, lawyers, counsellors and funeral directors.

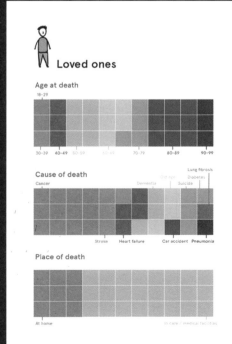

Loved ones

Age at death

Cause of death

Place of death

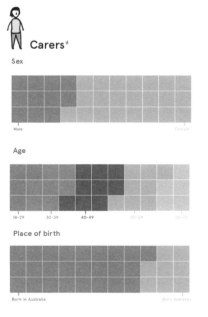

Carers

Sex

Age

Place of birth

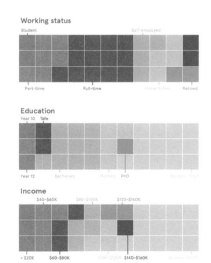

Working status

Education

Income

Understanding the experience

The aim was to uncover insights that could improve the role that government services play in this key life event, and to find opportunities to improve the experience for people in this often traumatic and difficult time.

The stories we uncovered highlighted the difficulties of dealing with expected and unexpected death, with death in cross-cultural situations (for example, an elderly relative from overseas dying whilst in Australia), the complexity of family dynamics (including will disputes), and the long-term effects on people's wellbeing of grief, trauma, and post-traumatic growth.

Representing complexity

Our research showed that there is no one-size-fits-all solution that can be applied to end-of-life care or what happens afterwards. Death happens to everyone — not just old people — and the circumstances can vary from foreseen to highly shocking and traumatic.

The services people need to access afterwards (such as applying for death certificates, making insurance claims, or closing accounts) are then delivered by specific departments and organisational groups with little to no integration. So, accessing each one can cause real pain and suffering at an already difficult time.

Chris Marmo is a design researcher and co-founder and CEO of Paper Giant. He holds a PhD in Cultural Geography & Ubiquitous Computing from RMIT University in Australia.

Paper Giant is a multi-disciplinary design studio based in Australia, that works across private, public and not-for-profit sectors to drive change towards a more just, fair and sustainable society, based in Melbourne. Paper Giant combines reséarch, design and strategy to create human-centred solutions to the complex problems that the world, people and organisations face.

Death
Hours — Minutes

The hours and minutes leading up to the medical death of an individual are vital. For illnesses, this often means intrusive medical intervention before death. Being present for a death is important and transformative for carers.

Absence

⚠ 5.2 Carers, above all, want to be present for the death of a loved one. Misinformation or unforeseen circumstances that lead to absence at the time of death become the source of ongoing trauma and guilt.

⚠ Medical intervention
5.1 Medical intervention that takes away control from carers or their loved ones leads to feelings of helplessness and anger. This is especially true when pain medication keeps loved ones unconscious in their final hours, compounding feelings of loss.

Accident or sudden death

Hidden illness

Suicide

The death of a loved one
What's it like to lose a loved one?

Case Study

Making meaning through faith

Elizabeth's husband and son died within two years of one another, only months after Elizabeth and her husband had moved from America to Australia. While she was still experiencing emotional distress, her religious beliefs enabled her to focus on positives aspects of her life.

"He passed October 21st 2013 and my son passed October 21st 2015. So I have an appointment with God to say what the hell were you thinking...I thank God up above, really to put me in on that street with those wonderful people...I say thank God I had him. How many women get what I had in a lifetime - all of us are guaranteed to die. We are. I got that figured out really strong in my head now."

The death of a loved one   41

Making it accessible

We also produced a detailed report that explored issues thematically, including 'what makes a good death?' and 'what's it like to lose a loved one?'. It included case studies that highlighted people's personal stories, as well as clear actions that governments and organisations could take to improve people's lives.

Together, both this report and the journey map form enduring foundational research, which has been shared widely, leading to strategic initiatives across Federal and State Governments in Australia.

"The six month struggle"

Death Administration
Days — Weeks — Months

This is the period of time immediately following the death of a loved one. It describes the process of certifying a death, and the formalities of enlisting service providers and beginning to close accounts, including ceasing government benefits the loved one may have been receiving.

Medical death certificate

The medical death certificate is required to have a funeral and to get the official death certificate

Hospital paperwork

The logistics required to handle a body that has recently been discovered is a source of trauma for carers. Support services are often insensitive.

Being informed by authorities

Dealing with a body

Coroner's report

If the death is accidental, sudden, or of an unknown cause, the coroner may need to be involved. This can take up to 4 months.

Lodging the death certificate

The medical death certificate can be lodged with Births, Deaths and Marriages online or via post. Usually it is the funeral director who does this.

Discovery

Telling people

Telling family and friends about an unexpected death is difficult, especially in traumatic circumstances, like a suicide.

Visualising service ecosystems

Conveying the complex nature
of services through visualising
'service ecosystems'

By Jesse Grimes

A 'service ecosystem' is — for me — the single most powerful deliverable in the service designer's arsenal to communicate the purpose and value of their craft. In this piece, I'd like to share how it's created and constructed, where in projects it can be applied, and what purposes it can serve. I think it makes most sense to begin with how a service ecosystem can lay the foundation for a successful service design or strategic design project.

In service design terminology, a 'service ecosystem' usually refers to the actors involved in a service, and the value exchanges that occur between them. A service ecosystem visualises the broad range of interactions and touchpoints that come into play across a customer lifecycle, and it does so with just a few layers of information. Yet despite its simple structure, it provides important new insights for the team that creates it.

Helping clarify the role and remit of service design

Despite the increasing recognition of service design, it's still not at all uncommon for an individual service designer to find themselves at the start of a project with a team who isn't entirely sure what their role is. Even in the largest organisations in which service design has earned a place in the design methodology, and service designers are assigned to each project, an individual service designer might often find themselves working with stakeholders and people from 'the business' that understand their role much less clearly than they do that of an interaction designer or a copywriter. This challenge of recognition can be even greater in settings where service design is entirely new, such as when a service design agency begins working with a new client.

When a service ecosystem is created towards the very beginning of a project, it effectively communicates the holistic nature of service design, thereby assisting the service designer in establishing their role and their way of thinking. In the earliest phases of a service design project, the 'service ecosystem' can be identified and visualised, long before more detailed customer journey mapping and service blueprinting work takes place. By building a shared understanding of the breadth and complexity of a service early-on, a service ecosystem is a powerful and easy-to-implement tool for the service designer's arsenal.

The structure of a service ecosystem

Like customer journey maps and service blueprints, a service ecosystem is a chronological view of a service experience, but it only concerns itself with phases, rather than the precise order of events within them. Within the phases, the user's needs are identified, alongside the service interactions, and the touchpoints on which they take place.

The circular visualisation is also created — and 'read' — in a clockwise manner. Let's start by looking at how it is structured.

A chronological view, captured in concentric rings

A service ecosystem is structured as a set of concentric rings, and one reads it clockwise from the '12 o'clock' position, phase-by-phase. This ring-based visualisation sets it apart from typical customer journey maps and service ecosystems, and also emphasises the fact that some service experiences don't fully end, but begin anew with the discovery and consumption of new products. It also emphasises the holistic nature of the ecosystem — encompassing all its elements within clear boundaries, as opposed to the sprawling, linear nature of blueprints and journeys.

Now let's have a look at the individual layers of information it contains, from the inside out.

User's need(s)

Representing the user-centred focus of service design, the service ecosystem places the user at the heart of the visualisation. The user's 'underlying need' occupies the very centre of the circle, while needs specific to individual phases are located in the relevant segments of the next ring outwards. Taking the example of a service ecosystem for an insurance provider, the underlying need for the user might be something like 'feel protected in case of the unexpected', or more succinctly, 'peace of mind'. During the 'usage' phase, in which an event occurs that triggers a claim, the more specific needs might be 'reassurance' and 'assistance'.

Interactions

The next ring outwards contains the discrete interactions the user has with the service, phrased in very simple, concrete terms (often 'verb + noun'). Within a segment of the 'Interactions' ring corresponding to a phase, no order is implied by where interactions are positioned; they are simply scattered through the segment. The interactions are also written without reference to a touchpoint, to avoid bogging down the document in unnecessary detail. Continuing the example of an insurance provider, interactions might be 'initiate claim' or 'change customer details' (not, 'report claim via app' or 'change address details in customer domain').

An additional benefit arises from identifying interactions in an agnostic manner within this ring. Because all of the in-use touchpoints are identified for a given phase, the service ecosystem can inform decisions on what interactions will be supported on what touchpoints. This can be done later, while scoping the functionality of the service (writing user stories or otherwise creating specifications), thanks to the generic way the interactions are written. By supporting the re-use of interactions across multiple touchpoints, the service can be built more efficiently, and also meet the needs of users who don't want to be confined to doing things only within one channel.

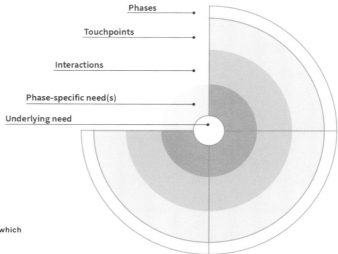

The elements of a service ecosystem, which are read in a clockwise manner.

Service and termination

Public website

App

WhatsApp

Email

Customer domain

Call centre

Terminate product

Change customer details

Change payment details

Change product coverages

Transparency

Speed

Awareness and orientation

Direct mail marketing

Social media

See Facebook ad

Public website

Email

Get quick quote

Receive marketing comms

Call centre

Well informed

Investigate product options

Insurance comparison site

Best value

Read product reviews

Consumer reviews site

Peace of mind

Clarity

Select product and coverages

Public website

Trust

Reassurance

Assistance

Ease

Set up customer details

Payment services provider

Customer domain

Resolution of claim

Policy documen-tation

Monitor claim progress

Set up payment details

Email

Email

Describe loss

Receive proof of coverage

Call centre

Call centre

Indicate claim

App

WhatsApp

App

App

Usage

Insurance certificate

Public website

Purchase and on-boarding

An example of a high-level service ecosystem for an insurance provider.

Touchpoints

The places on which the interactions of a given phase occur are gathered together in the next ring outwards: 'Touchpoints'. Here, touchpoints that play a role in a specific phase are named. They could be things such as 'app' or 'call centre', or 'email newsletter'. Similarly to interactions, no order is implied by where they are positioned in the ring, and no attempt is made to visually link interactions and touchpoints. Finding the right level of detail when describing touchpoints is also important. 'Online', 'digital' or 'face-to-face' would be too vague to be of use. 'Public website' is acceptable, but there may be even more value for naming specific aspects of that website as well, such as 'customer support forum'.

Phases

The outermost ring is self-explanatory — it contains the high-level phases of the service that the user progresses through. In practice, these phase names should correspond with phases used in later deliverables, such as customer journey maps. For many services, typical phase names will suffice (e.g. 'awareness', 'orientation', 'purchase', 'use', etc.). It often makes sense to identify the phase names in advance of the service ecosystem workshop, to kick-start its creation.

A word about granularity

It is tempting — especially with experience creating detailed customer journeys and service blueprints — to go into a great level of detail when creating a service ecosystem. However, this risks creating an unwieldy and overly-complex document, which will require significant time to create and interpret. Much as in customer journey mapping, a significant proportion of the value delivered by a service ecosystem comes about in the awareness and discussions it triggers within the team during its creation, and not simply the deliverable itself.

For an interaction, 'pay bill' is adequate; it is not necessary to reveal further complexity by having individual interactions for 'pay bill by credit card' and 'pay bill by direct debit', for example. Similarly, avoid getting too detailed when identifying touchpoints and phases.

When to create a service ecosystem

With the structure out of the way, I'd like to move on to when and how to create the visualisation itself. There are two possible moments within a project to bring together a team to create a service ecosystem, and each has a different purpose:

At the start of a project

At the very start of a project, creating a service ecosystem helps to highlight the potential complexity of the service that's being designed, or redesigned. Typically, project teams start their work with a relatively 'blinkered' view of their service. However, creating a service ecosystem very early on confronts the team with realities that they may not have adequately considered. Rather than viewing their app being used in isolation, for example, they might come to realise it exists within a much larger context for the end user.

Furthermore, they become aware of the chronological nature of the service experience, with its different phases, and different touchpoints in use over time. When employed this early on in a project, it's important to keep in mind that the service being visualised is based on conjecture and assumption. Nonetheless, it can very powerfully demonstrate the holistic perspective that service design takes, thereby building the case for service design. In fact, in my work with start-ups, it's the very first service design activity I carry out.

To visualise insights from the 'discovery' phase

A service ecosystem can also be employed to visualise the current state of a service, based on insights derived from research. In this case, it joins personas and 'as-is' customer journeys as a way to document the service experience at a high level.

The value of a service ecosystem

By systematically working through each phase of a service and identifying the touchpoints and interactions that come into play, a team often realises that things are — or will be — more complex and interconnected than they had previously thought. And in cases where ownership and delivery of different elements of a service are spread among people or departments — such as channels or products — the creation of this simply-structured visualisation can have an especially great impact.

I have facilitated more than a few service ecosystem creation workshops in which individual product owners were for the first time confronted with the fact that their 'product' existed alongside many other touchpoints that the end customers will end up using as well, not to mention the third-party touchpoints that still play a key role in the overall service experience.

Triggering this holistic 'service' awareness, as the first step towards the eventual orchestration of all the touchpoints and interactions, is the true power of the service ecosystem.

But beyond surfacing the complexity of a service, a service ecosystem can also be used for more concrete purposes, which I will get to a little later.

How to create a service ecosystem

So what does it take to draw a service ecosystem — whether 'as-is' or 'to-be'? Firstly, it's a team effort, rather than something crafted by a solo service designer. Identify a group of people who are responsible for the service, and invite them to a workshop. Strategic and ownership roles tend to bring the most value to the activity. Unlike customer journey mapping and service blueprinting, the specific insights of policy, legal, marketing or IT representatives — for example — are less relevant here.

Working on a whiteboard or wall which can be later dedicated to the service ecosystem is ideal. If that's not possible, two easel/A0-size pieces of paper taped together can be a good start. Start by drawing and labelling the relevant rings, and identify the phase names on Post-its. Distribute them around the outside of the outermost ring, but be prepared to reposition them based on the eventual size of each phase.

If customer research has been carried out already, it should be possible to identify the needs at the centre of the visualisation. If not, you can consider making assumptions of the needs, or leaving them blank until they can be filled in based on real insights (and then used to sense-check the interactions and touchpoints). If assumptions are made concerning needs, ensure they remain recognised as such, and are replaced with validated needs once research has taken place.

Then continue to fill in the interactions and touchpoints, on a phase-by-phase basis. Normally, the team members present, and the knowledge they bring, is enough to accurately capture the true extent of touchpoints and interactions. Although the service ecosystem is not intended to replace ideation activities later in a project, it can be employed at the earliest stages of a project and help identify expected functionality of the future service, and where opportunities might exist.

In general, a 90-minute workshop is adequate to complete a service ecosystem. For complex services, or cases where progress moves slowly due to lots of discussions, a second 90-minute workshop may be necessary.

New insights through additional annotations

A service ecosystem's real value comes in the insights it delivers for visualising future services, but it can also be employed to bring current services into focus in a new way. This can be useful to see the impact of future changes to the service.

Three additional types of annotation can be used when creating the service ecosystem, to bring in additional layers of information:

- Obsolete touchpoints and interactions: A line can be drawn through items to show that in the future, they will no longer play a role in the service experience. This is useful for seeing the evolving complexity of a service, transitions between channels, and highlighting those that are new.
- Third-party touchpoints and interactions: These can be indicated with brackets surrounding the item, to show that the specified touchpoint is beyond the control of the service provider. This is useful to provide context when third parties still (significantly) impact the overall service experience, such as the role of an auto repair garage in relation to car insurance.
- Releases and future functionality: When visualising a 'to-be' service, visual distinctions can be made between different product releases. For example, a different colour can be used to indicate interactions which won't be available at launch, but later in time.

Harnessing the power of a service ecosystem

In addition to the insights that the creation of a service ecosystem delivers, it can also have more practical applications within a (service design) project. Here are several ways in which the information and insights it contains can be translated into action:

As a precursor to customer journey mapping

Although customer journey mapping is ideally done for an entire service lifecycle, practical considerations often mean that journeys are shortened to encompass only parts of the service experience. A service ecosystem can be used to identify individual, shorter journeys, by grouping sets of interactions that span one or more phases. With the journey identified, the requisite research and mapping activities can occur later.

To identify areas of opportunity

A completed service ecosystem makes visible the type and numbers of interactions in the experience lifecycle. In doing so, it also lays bare the stretches of time where no interactions take place, or perhaps where touchpoints are over- or under-utilised. Insights such as these can be the trigger to determine whether new elements of the service should be introduced.

For competitor analysis

When designing a new service, a deep understanding of what's on offer from competitors is important. Based on simple research methods such as 'mystery shopping', it's possible to easily gather enough input to visualise the service ecosystem of the competitor. Analysing theirs and yours side by side will make visible key points of difference, and might help trigger innovation.

To support the orchestration of complex services

Complex services — especially those delivered by large organisations — demand orchestration at a strategic level. This orchestration can be supported by the holistic perspective a service ecosystem affords. Rather than having touchpoints developed and managed individually, teams and managerial roles can refer to the service ecosystem when planning work, to ensure the "big picture" of the service experience is kept in perspective.

A service ecosystem requires a relatively low investment of time and effort, yet pays quick dividends, especially for those seeking to convince stakeholders of the value that service design can bring. And it can remain a living document, updated as required, and used to communicate the totality of a service, in a way well-known deliverables like customer journey maps sometimes fail to do.

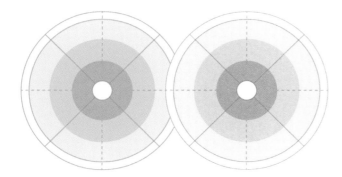

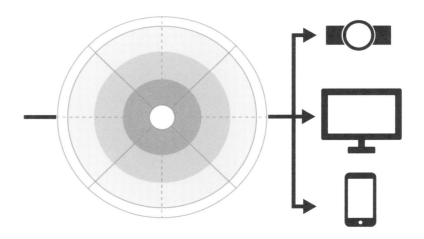

Jesse Grimes is a freelance service designer, with thirteen years' experience in the field and has worked as a design consultant since 1998. He's now based in Amsterdam and works for clients nationally and internationally. Jesse's work includes a wide range of global brands and he has specific expertise in the financial sector and in working for start-ups and innovation contexts, as well as being a coach, trainer and workshop facilitator. His current clients include a multinational in the agriculture sector, as well as a Berlin-based cleantech start-up and a blockchain-based social impact start-up in The Hague. Jesse is also Senior Vice President of the global Service Design Network, Editor-in-Chief of its journal, Touchpoint and co-founder and Head of Training of the SDN Academy. Jesse regularly organizes and speaks at national and international events for the service design community and contributes to the development of the service design discipline through his writing, speaking and interviews.

Case study
Draw and discover

Sketching and mapping as a versatile tool across research stages

By Sophie Knight and Bas Raijmakers (STBY)

Mapping is a vital and versatile tool for designers. It goes much further than merely communicating something to a viewer or reader. At STBY we often draw, sketch, and map — and we see that it helps us achieve multiple objectives at once.

For instance, while conducting research for the What Design Can Do Clean Energy Challenge[1], which spanned five cities on five continents in 2018-2019, we used mapping extensively. It was a process of experimentation and iteration, and mapping helped us to make sense of things and bring the team onto the same page.

When drawing the maps for the challenge, there was lots of trial and error — we didn't come up with the final versions straight away. The maps functioned much like drafts of a text: we improved them over time, refining with each version. We used the maps as a way to make sense of things and to have conversations together after doing individual research.

Mapping to create a perspective
When we began the research for the Clean Energy Challenge, we had to identify the most serious global energy issues, as well as the specific challenges in each of the five cities: São Paulo, Delhi, Mexico City, Nairobi, and Amsterdam.

Kate Raworth's book *Doughnut Economics*[2] had just been published and was causing a storm. Raworth's 'doughnut' was a diagram representing a sustainable and just economy, with the hole at the centre representing a basic social foundation and the space

beyond the doughnut representing the environmental consequences of using too many resources, which she called 'overshoot'. The goal is to have an economy within the doughnut: we have to consume fewer resources, but not so little that we erode people's access to water, food, education, and so on.

While Raworth's version represented the entire economy, we started experimenting with the diagram to illustrate a just and sustainable use of energy, creating what we called the 'energy bagel'. In the centre was energy poverty, and at the outer boundary the excessive use of fossil fuels, which we called 'carbon decadence' (see first sketch on opposite page, at the top left). Obviously, inside the doughnut is where

we should be: consuming the necessary amount of energy to uphold quality of life for all, but not so much fossil fuel energy that we aggravate climate change, air pollution, and other problems.

To explore this idea, we made several versions, changing the parameters and the concepts expressed. For example, the second

Below: In a diagram that we sketched in addition to the energy bagel, we tried to map the flow of consequences, to help us understand where designers could make a difference and what part of the problem designers could focus on. Making this map made it clear that although there were some things that designers may not be able to change (such as storms), they could tackle the consequences of those phenomena.

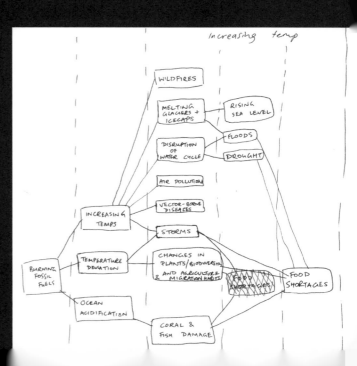

The energy bagel

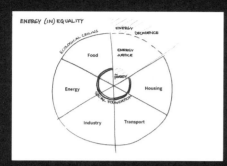

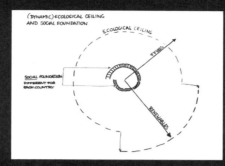

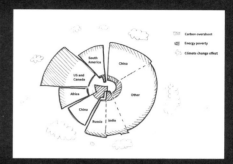

We used Kate Raworth's 'Doughnut Economics' as a model and built an 'energy bagel' on top of it: energy poverty in the middle, or the 'shortfall', and carbon decadence on the outside, as the 'excess'

We translated academic concepts such as 'energy justice' and 'fuel poverty' into visual representations

We used the same 'doughnut' shape to illustrate the mismatch between (greenhouse gas) contributions to climate change versus the consequences that countries will suffer. India had the biggest disparity between these two

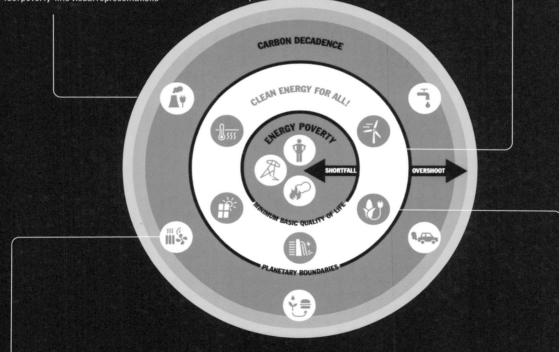

We illustrated the 'nexus' of each problem in each city. For example, in Delhi, the housing-energy nexus (icons in outer layer)

We used icons to symbolise various things that energy is used for, e.g. heating, cooling, mobility, food and mapped these onto each of the five cities to see what problems the cities had in common and which problems came up most often

sketch at the right illustrates our realisation that the boundaries are flexible: the amount of energy required to provide a social foundation differs by region or country; and the amount of energy it takes to hit the ecological ceiling differs depending on the type of energy (oil will get you there faster than wind power).

Mapping to understand differences and dependencies

In our research we had found that some of the regions with the lowest per-capita energy consumption and the most fragile social foundations were, unfairly, going to suffer the most from climate change. Asia topped this category. North America, by contrast, had the highest energy consumption per-capita but was projected to be less affected by climate change, relative to the other regions.

We sketched out a different version of the energy bagel to illustrate this (see one version at the top right on previous page), with the size of the clouds representing the weight of the climate change consequences. This was an attempt to communicate the notion of energy justice, which is a state in which the costs and benefits of energy production and consumption are equally shared among all.

In this version of the doughnut we also showed how much of a shortfall each region had on their social foundations, versus their excessive use of fossil fuel energy. Asia had the biggest gap in its social foundation, and the smallest overshoot.

While we could have theoretically grasped the idea through reading or looking at figures, mapping it made it instantly comprehensible. We could see which aspects of the issue we should ask designers to focus on, and we could understand why it feels unfair to ask people in India to cut back on fossil fuels if it decreases quality of life, while those in North America and Europe consume far larger amounts and have long enjoyed a higher standard of living.

Mapping to create an inclusive language

Making the maps helped the research team to make sense of the sources we were finding and to communicate

separate sources, the maps we made were a vital tool in updating each other on what we had read and learned elsewhere. They also helped us to analyse and synthesise the data and information we were finding.

But the maps we made weren't simply sketches to help the STBY team understand each other. They also greatly aided us in meetings with What Design Can Do and IKEA Foundation, the main funder of the challenge. What would have taken a few minutes to explain verbally could be communicated instantly, helping the rest of the team to reflect and give their input rapidly.

The maps we used steered our story and helped to build shared understanding between a project team of people with backgrounds as diverse as advertising, design, journalism, academic research, climate action funding, and policy. The maps served as an inclusive language and became a powerful internal tool for communication well before we tried to communicate our findings to the wider

Mapping to combine diverse sources of information

One of the challenges we faced was pulling together information from multiple sources in very different styles. From news articles written in plain language to densely referenced IPCC reports and policy reports, our sources spanned a wide range of disciplines. Putting all these sources into a single text report was difficult, as the style had to be coherent. Mapping the information, however, effectively smoothes out the irregularities between the sources and makes it instantly comprehensible.

This helped enormously when we condensed lots of desk research into maps that showed the main energy problems each city struggles with, and the connections between those problems. We then better understood cause and effect in each city, and together with the team, we were able to identify the areas we could ask designers to focus on, and what problems they might tackle in those areas.

VALUE MAP

ADDITIONAL BENEFITS FOR PEOPLE (e.g. cost, social inclusion)

SWEET SPOT
Also think about:
- Relevance
- Impact
- Feasibility
- Excitement
- Scalability

CLEAN AND GREEN ENERGY FOR ALL

Above: We also used other types of maps, as collaboration tools, in stakeholder workshops that we ran before launching the challenge. In each city we invited a diverse group of people to take part in the workshops, from policymakers to architects and NGOs. We asked them to map out the most pressing issues in their cities related to Clean Energy, which helped to create a consensus among participants and enable them to draw out insights.

Mapping to communicate insights to a wider audience

Perhaps one of the widely understood functions of a map is communication to non-specialists. Making a map requires a lot of skill and knowledge; the mapmaker must gather and arrange enormous amounts of data before whittling it down to the clear representation that you see on a map. Reading a map, fortunately, does not require this level of expertise.

That's why maps were a perfect tool to communicate our findings from scientific, technical, and political reports to designers. They then didn't need to dig into lengthy reports to find the insights they needed; the map would show them the way, and allowed them to get a good grasp of the main clean energy issues at play for each city.

After making the sketches of the problems in each city, we made refined versions for the final briefing packs for the Clean Energy Challenge. These highlighted the main problems we wanted designers to focus on, and the opportunities that these offered to designers in particular.

While creating briefs from scratch can be a challenge, creating the final maps with the design team at What Design Can Do was relatively straightforward — because we had so many sketches to work from, and had built up conversations about the maps over the many weeks of meetings during the research phase. In that sense, the maps in the published briefing packs for the Clean Energy Challenge are effectively the final iteration of the mapping that started right at the beginning of the research.

As you can see, maps are not simply the polished product marking the culmination of research; they are part of the exploration, discovery and collaboration of research itself.

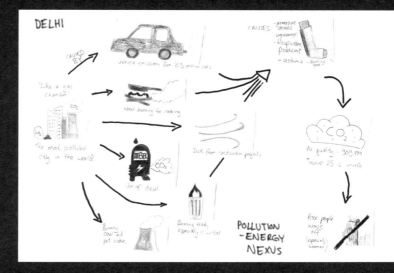

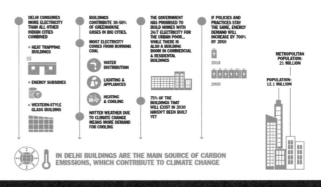

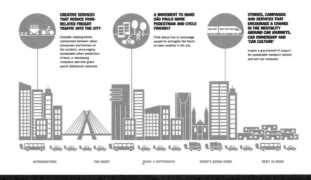

1 https://cleanenergychallenge.whatdesigncando.com/

2 Raworth, Kate. *Doughnut Economics*. Cornerstone, 2017

Bas Raijmakers is co-founder and Creative Director of STBY in London and Amsterdam, working for clients in the public sector and industry. Bas has a background in cultural studies, the early internet industry and interaction design. He holds a PhD in Design Interactions from the Royal College of Art, in London.

Sophie Knight is a journalist and researcher based in Amsterdam focusing on climate change and the intersection of people, culture and their environment. Her work has been published in The Financial Times, WIRED UK, The Guardian, and The Japan Times. As a design researcher she has worked in Japan, the Netherlands and Zimbabwe for STBY and Studio D Radiodurans.

Getting on the same page

Bridging boundaries through mapping

By Michael Johnson (Glasgow School of Art)
and Megan Anderson (STBY)

In the fields of design research and service design, maps can serve all sorts of functions. They make implicit knowledge explicit, they illustrate and simplify complex journeys, and they highlight knowledge gaps and service shortcomings. But a lot of the value that maps provide manifests around the object itself: before, during, and after it is created. The proliferation of design across disciplinary boundaries, where designers cannot claim contextual expertise, can lead to many layers of abstraction in the communication and practice of design. Mapping approaches are often developed or used to re-orientate and coordinate such collaborative design processes.

Various service design scholars have studied and articulated the power of mapping in terms of enabling engagement, participation, coordination and collaboration across disciplines and diverse stakeholder groups. The concept of 'design artefact' and the notion of 'boundary object' help us think of maps as mechanisms that enable these social processes. In this way, 'mapping' is more than 'map-making', and requires a unique skill set beyond just graphic design. Participatory research, co-creative workshop facilitation, stakeholder engagement, and even conflict management are important skills for mapping in design research. Maps help bridge boundaries, and co-create shared language throughout multi-stakeholder innovation projects. In essence, they allow us to get — and stay — on the same page (pun intended).

Inviting interactions with the design problem

Maps can be seen as design artefacts defined by Thomas Binder et al.[1], alongside other entities like sketches, diagrams, representations, storyboards, models and prototypes, constitutive of the 'object of design', or 'design thing'. For design artefacts to have value and significance, they have to become part of the living experience of human beings in the way these afford, invite, and oblige interactions. These artefacts are not the object being designed per se, but each of them allows designers to interact with the design problem, and discuss its different features with various stakeholders[2].

Drawing things together

Designing is thus presented as a social act of 'drawing things together', a framing of design competence that seeks to tap into the existing tacit knowledge of user participation as 'design-by-doing'[3], while also permitting different perspectives and actors 'to engage in alignments of their conflicting objects of design'[4]. This frames design competence through the ability and use of design artefacts to objectify, articulate and challenge assumptions across disciplinary boundaries in the design process.

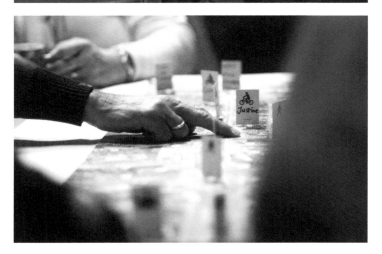

A means of translation

The complementary concept of 'boundary objects' was initially developed by Sociologists Susan Leigh Star and James R. Griesemer to describe objects that have different meanings in different social worlds, but a structure that is common enough to make them recognizable across groups[5]. They are a 'means of translation' and their creation and management is key in 'developing and maintaining coherence across intersecting social worlds'.

Building on this, Etienne Wenger describes boundary objects as entities that can link 'communities of practice' together as they allow different groups to collaborate on a common task. This denotes boundaries as a 'shared space'[6] between disciplines, where coordination can take place without consensus and local understandings can be reframed in the context of a wider collective activity[7]. Artefacts, such as maps, can mediate different forms of participation and build collective identities to orient communities and align with other processes (Wenger, 2010: 184). They also make shared progress more real and act as a guide for collective learning through a process of reification[8].

Empowering inter-disciplinary communities

It is through these lenses that maps can be recognised as crucial sites and mechanisms of participation and progression, and where design innovation can be argued to take place. The more abstract and ill-defined a map, the more its meaning has to be coordinated anew, and understanding it (in terms of use) becomes increasingly similar to designing[9]. Identifying maps as boundary objects reveals a collective process of sense-making and the need to foster design competencies that can empower interdisciplinary communities of practice as the norm.

In recent years, STBY has been commissioned by various local councils in Amsterdam to help them engage residents in the early stages of public space (re)design projects. We have developed a customised research approach for this called 'Street Labs'. In these Labs, table-top neighbourhood maps are the centerpiece of discussion for groups of local residents, business owners and local government representatives. The maps provide a familiar starting point for everyone and allow diverse groups of people to add unique personal perspectives and experiences of neighbourhood spaces. They also foster collective and constructive dialogue around how and why things could change.

Developing a shared understanding of a personal experience: For a project about diabetes, STBY designed a tabletop ecosystem map to foster conversations around support networks for those with the disease. We designed various icons to represent human and non-human support actors. Participants 'plotted' these various actors on a map, while explaining who and what they were, how they connect and how they provide support (or fail to). By the end of these 2-hour conversations, the researchers and participants developed clear, visual indications of where and how support could be improved or better connected in specific contexts.

Dr Michael Pierre Johnson is a post-doctoral design researcher, with experience in ethnographic research and design-led approaches to inform product, digital, service and organisational innovation. Since gaining his PhD through the AHRC-funded knowledge exchange hub Design in Action in 2016, Michael has since been working in multiple projects of collaborative creative engagement, which in Jan 2019 led to him being awarded an AHRC funded Innovation Leadership Fellowship in the Creative Economy. His research interests are on making the effects and viability of Design Innovation approaches, and the preferable changes they seek to serve, more explicit within complex collaborative contexts through visual mapping methods.

1 Thomas Binder, Giorgio De Michelis, Pelle Ehn, Giulio Jacucci, Per Linde and Ina Wagner, Design Things, (MIT Press, 2011).

2 Binder, Design Things, 59.

3 Pelle Ehn, Participation in design things, (Indiana University, In Proceedings of the tenth anniversary conference on participatory design, 2008), 92-101.

4 Thomas Binder, Giorgio De Michelis, Pelle Ehn, Giulio Jacucci, Per Linde and Ina Wagner, What is the object of design?, CHI'12 Extended Abstracts on Human Factors in Computing Systems, (Austin, ACM, 2012): 25.

5 Susan L. Star and James R. Griesemer, Institutional Ecology, `Translations' and Boundary Objects: Amateurs and Professionals in Berkeley's Museum of Vertebrate Zoology, 1907-39, Social Studies of Science 19, No. 3, (Sage, August 1989): 393.

6 Susan L. Star, This is not a boundary object: Reflections on the origin of a concept, Science, Technology & Human Values 35, No.5, (September 2010): 601 - 617.

7 Beth A. Bechky, Sharing Meaning across Occupational Communities: The Transformation of Understanding on a Production Floor, Organization Science 14, No. 3 (Informs, May - June, 2003): 312-330.

8 Etienne Wenger, Communities of Practice and Social Learning Systems: the Career of a Concept, Social Learning Systems and Communities of Practice, (London, Springer, 2010): 180.

9 Katharina Bredies, Rosan Chow, and Gesche Joost, Addressing Use as Design: A Comparison of Constructivist Design Approaches, The Design Journal 13, No. 2 (July, 2010): 159.

Case study
Mapping the invisible

Visualising the process and value of design

By Cat Drew (Design Council)

Part of mapping is to create visibility so people can value something and act on it. In this way, the Double Diamond, alongside any other process diagram, can be seen as a map. It was created by Design Council staff between the years 2000 and 2004, by looking at how a range of design-intensive firms were using design, as well as internal projects around design and education, and design and technology[1]. At the time Richard Eiserman said, "there is no single design process diagram". So the team, led by Chris Vanstone and Anna White set about creating one.

The power of simplicity
The first visualisation, sketched on a napkin, was an attempt to simply visualise what was to many a mysterious and invisible process. Divergent and convergent thinking had been around

from the 1960s (with Victor Papanek drawing them in his 1960 *Design for the Real World*), but what was new was the 'first diamond' space, and the importance of taking time to understand a range of perspectives and reframe a challenge. According to Andrea Cooper, by visualising the design and discover phases enabled designers to communicate the importance of these early stage activities. In turn, it opened up funding for early-stage design research.

15 years later, Design Council celebrated its 75th birthday and we reflected on the process that has proved valuable for designers and non-designers alike, being used all over the world with over 600 million hits. We asked people where it was useful and where it had limitations. Its simplicity is both a strength and

a weakness. By scaling out to make something comprehensible, it loses the complexity and the messiness. It is not as linear as it looks, and it does not show all the things that happen around a single innovation to make it land. And of course as design is being asked to work on more complex challenges, we know that a single innovation will never be enough.

Napkin sketches
In Toronto, at the Service Design Global Conference 2019, I asked around 80 service designers to draw the missing, invisible activity that happens around the edges of the Double Diamond process. I handed out a stack of napkins, and asked them to visualise these in a simple, understandable way. They drew sketches and symbols to represent: relationships (building trust

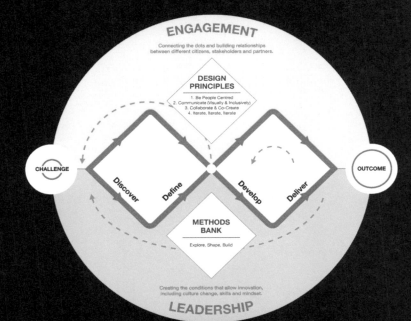

The new Double Diamond model: Framework for innovation © Design Council 2019

and confidence with stakeholders, learning and onboarding of those new to the design process, and managing conflicts that arise during the process), implementation (recognising that design is a continuous process of iteration and redesign), leadership and measuring impact (including what didn't happen), engagement (and shifting power and equity to those engaged in the design process). These are all essential for change to happen, but generally in client work, we never leave enough space, resources, and energy for this important work, out of which the design should emerge.

The invisible value of design

The other thing that is often invisible in the design process is all the intangible value that is created that does not neatly count into economic gains, savings or social and environmental value, which has more varied measurements still. Linked to this wider activity of engaging stakeholders and of empowering citizens is a wider ripple effect of value: reframing how we see issues, opening up imagination spaces for others to develop their own ideas, building connections and relationships that go on to spark further innovations, and giving confidence to someone to be more active in their own role. All of these things are valuable, but because we haven't mapped them and made them visible, we don't measure them. They are not seen, and not valued. As part of our next iteration of The Design Economy, the Design Council's report on the state of design in the UK, we are going to start measuring the 'invisible value' of design. This time, it will be mapped for others loud and clear.

Participants at the 2019 Service Design Global Conference in Toronto draw the missing, invisible activity that happens around the edges of the Double Diamond process.

Cat Drew is the Chief Design Officer at Design Council where she brings together architecture and the built environment, public sector design and business innovation to support people live healthier, happier and safer lives. Previously, Cat has held leadership positions at FutureGov and Uscreates, was a co-founder of the UK Government's Policy Lab, and combines 10 years of experience in Government with an MA in Graphic Design. She speaks widely about the value of design and co-presents BBC Radio 4 The Fix.

1 There are also a wider number of names associated with the Double Diamond — they are: Clive Grinyer, Jonathan Ball, Gill Wildman, Jennie Winhall, Anna White, Sonja Dahl, Andrea Cooper, Chris Vanstone, Jeremy Walker, Neil Gridley, Max Bielenberg, Anna Richell, Richelle Harun, Aviv Katz, Lesley Morris, Tamsin Smith and others

Foreign Lands

The wonderful world of maps

A journey across mapping practices

By Megan Anderson (STBY)

The word *map* tends to be used quite loosely, and can refer to all sorts of maps, charts, diagrams and schematics that seek to visualise a range of complex systems. It is most often associated with the visualisation of a particular spatial area, with roots in the Medieval Latin word *mappa mundi*, meaning "map of the world". The first element, *mappa*, comes from Latin meaning 'napkin, cloth', on which maps were drawn. A word often used synonymously with *map* is *chart*. Interestingly, this term has similar etymological roots, in the Latin word *charta* or 'paper, papyrus leaf'. The term *diagram* is more precisely defined by what it is, rather than the medium upon which it exists. It comes from the Greek word *diagramma*, meaning 'a geometric figure, that which is marked out by lines'.

Colloquially, these terms have come to be used synonymously in many cases. Across disciplines, many of these terms are used interchangeably and there are no clear distinctions in the way that they are used. It is important to note that there are distinctions between what is mapped (or charted, diagrammed etc.), how it is mapped, and why.

How many maps, in the descriptive or geographical sense might be needed to deal exhaustively with a given space, to code and decode all of its meanings and contents?

Henri Lefebvre, from *"The Production of Space,"* 1991

Mapping as a universal language

You could say that anything could and has been mapped or diagrammed: space, time, objects, stories, processes, organisations. These entities can all be considered systems, and all systems can be visualised in one way or another. There are various factors that dictate how a system is visualised though. These include how much the 'mapmaker' knows about the system, why the system is being visualised and for whom (i.e. the 'agenda' of the map), the medium of the visualisation (e.g. cloth, papyrus, computer screen, tabletop, etc.), and the skills, techniques, and disciplinary rules and traditions influencing the mapmaker.

Maps also differ significantly in terms of abstraction. Some maps are more literal and detailed in the way that they visualise a system. In these cases the objective of the map is often to provide enough detail for the audience to be guided through space or time in some specific way: for navigation across land, sea or sky, for example. Or to build something in a particular way, like the IKEA diagrams we all know and love. Interestingly, seafarers distinguish charts from maps in this way. For them, a chart is more than a map and is defined by its more specific function: to help mariners plot courses through open bodies of water with hydrographic data like information on water depths, shoreline, tide predictions, obstructions to navigation such as rocks and shipwrecks, and navigational aids. Maps do not have this level of functional detail in the eyes of a sailor.

Other geographical maps do not have spatial navigation as their 'agenda' at all. Rather, their objective is to visualise other types of information like territory, soil type, climate, land use or subsurface structures. These types of maps typically still seek to represent land (or space) with respect to scale and accuracy, but purposefully omit the type of information that a navigation chart might include. Other maps deliberately distort scale or omit information to better serve the function of the map.

Most maps of geographical things in space, although often abstracted, distorted and subjective, still aim to represent tangible systems, objects, and relationships that exist in the physical world. There are other disciplines, like architecture and engineering that visualise tangible systems too, even if they might not exist in the real world yet. But some maps and diagrams deal with systems, concepts, processes, and relationships that are much more abstract, invisible, or intangible: knowledge like history, senses, ideas, and organisational processes. And there are some maps that seek not to reflect any type of reality at all. These are maps of fantasy realms and fictional tales, utopian speculations and imagined futures.

There are many great books out there on the history of various different types of maps and information visualisation: from maps of space and time, to scientific diagrams and maps of the imagination. Rather than attempting to do what others have already done very well, the primary aim here is to illustrate how humans have historically mapped all sorts of things. No one discipline or person can lay claim to the 'invention' of mapping or the map. Mapping is a universal practice that has benefitted all societies and disciplines. In fact, many maps have acted as bridges between disciplines, merging and layering various types of knowledge to solve problems, guide others, or inspire change or reflection.

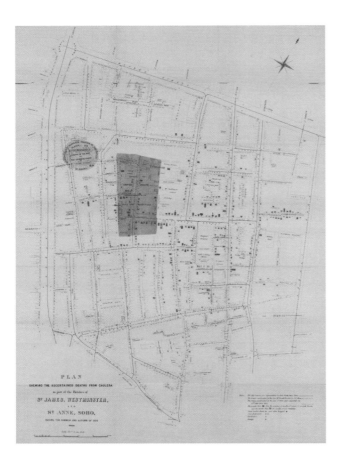

Above: This celestial map by the Dutch cartographer and artist Frederik de Wit (1670) beautifully shows solar orbits, the lunar phases, as well as the constellations visible from earth. De Wit is actually most known for his city maps, world maps and atlases, and his map-making company flourished during the Dutch Golden Age. In the 16th and 17th centuries, Dutch-speaking cartographers helped lay the foundations for the birth and development of modern cartography, including nautical cartography and celestial cartography.

Left: This famous map made by John Snow shows the distribution of deaths from the 1854 outbreak of cholera in London. It is known for attributing the spread of cholera to contaminated water, rather than air as previously believed. This is a great example of the power of thematic maps (dot distribution maps in particular) in combining geospatial data with other data forms to find meaningful patterns.

Maps of space

Geographical maps are perhaps most commonly conjured when the word 'map' is even mentioned. Humans have been mapping space, including land, sea, and sky for millennia. Over the years the mapping of these entities has resulted in a specialist discipline: cartography, the science or art of making or drawing maps[1]. Cartography has many fringes and includes various map types. Celestial cartography, also called uranography, is the branch of astronomy concerned with the description and mapping of the stars, galaxies, and other astronomical objects[2].

There are many different types and scales of more earthly maps. People often distinguish between 'general reference maps', 'thematic maps' and 'cartometric maps', though in reality most maps are hybrids[3]. General reference maps have features of the earth's surface, like mountains, rivers, oceans, roads, and buildings. They seek to show spatial relationships and relative location only. Thematic maps focus on a particular topic (like population density or cases of infection) as it relates to a particular geographic area. The geographic base data tends to be secondary, or related to another form of data. There are also special purpose cartometric maps, which fall amidst the blurry lines between general and thematic maps. These types of maps are often industry related and combine general map elements with thematic attributes for tasks requiring accurate distance calculations, such as surveying, hiking, and resource management[4].

Another useful distinction is between topographic and topological maps. Whereas topographic maps detail the realistic shape and features of land surfaces, topological maps are more general and disregard scale in the interest of other types of information. Public transportation maps are good examples of topological maps.

Public transportation maps are examples of topological maps. Their goal is to help people quickly and easily navigate complex transit systems. Therefore, they tend to prioritise clear and simple graphics, over topographic detail. These types of maps illustrate well the importance of understanding the audience and their needs when designing maps. The New York City Subway Map has been at the centre of many debates around this topic. There were famous debates in 1978 between graphic designer Massimo Vignelli's with his modernist, diagrammatic map [left] , and John Tauranac and Michael Hertzs' more geographic version [right]. Which one do you think is more fit for purpose?

Maps of people (bodies, families, organisations)

The field of medicine has benefitted hugely from the practice of mapping. John Snow and his map of the London cholera outbreak brought him the status of one of the world's first epidemiologists. But there are other kinds of maps that zoom in from a bird's-eye view, and focus just on the human body and the complexity of subsystems within.

The Ayurvedic Man is perhaps one of the most ancient examples of how the human body has been mapped and is the manifestation of early medical understanding and healing practices in the world. Early South Asian anatomical maps evoke a poetic conception of the body widely held in the day; charting emotions, blockages, chakras and metaphysical energies[5]. As medicine and technology have co-advanced, our knowledge of the human body, the organs, tissues, muscles, and cells within have become much more advanced and our maps have evolved to become a lot more granular.

Zooming out of the body, we can start looking at collectives of bodies: families and organisations. Family trees and organisational charts have been common ways to map these entities. Family trees, also called pedigree charts or genograms, have been typical ways that genealogical data has been represented. Historically, family trees were used to map the kinship and descent of rulers and nobles, and prove claims to wealth and power. In recent times, with the rise of personal genealogical DNA

testing, everyone can map their genealogy. Rather than for claims to wealth and money, family trees of today help people understand their personal histories and connect with long-lost family members.

Families and tribes are one of the many scales at which human organisational activity has been mapped. Visualising organisational activity and the division of labour at broader societal levels has also been a practice dating back to ancient times. Societies, militaries, public bodies, and enterprises have all been mapped in various ways. The ballooning bureaucracies born in the Industrial Age necessitated forms of sensemaking to create shared awareness of — and control over — emergent complex organisational structures and relationships. From here, the modern organisational chart as we know it was born.

Many mammoth bureaucracies of the day mapped themselves in various forms, most commonly in terms of function or division; detailing roles, relationships, and hierarchies therein. The static organisational chart served its purpose for slower moving times. But in today's fast-moving, networked age this format has been criticised as outdated[6] and unhelpful[7]. At the same time, companies are experimenting with new organisational forms giving rise to post-bureaucratic forms of organising. If mapped, these look quite different to the organisational charts of the 19th and 20th centuries.

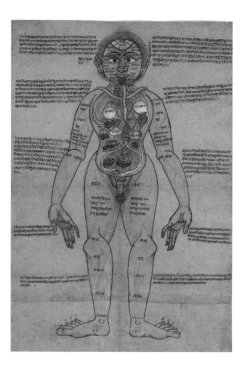

An 18th-century Nepali painting called the Ayurvedic Man showing the organs and vessels of the male body according to Ayurveda, a centuries-old, but ever evolving set of medical practices translating to the "knowledge of long life".

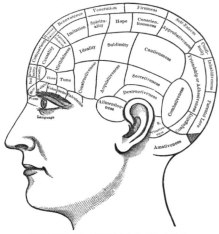

A phrenological chart published in 1859 in the The Illustrated Self-Instructor in Phrenology and Physiology. Korbinian Brodmann, a German neurologist, was the first and most well known "brain mapper" of the early 1900's. He mapped what came to be known as Brodmann areas, based on his observations of the cytoarchitectural organization in the cerebral cortex. Through this, he was able to illustrate his early hypothesis: the cerebral cortex had different mixes of cells, indicating that each region might differ in function.

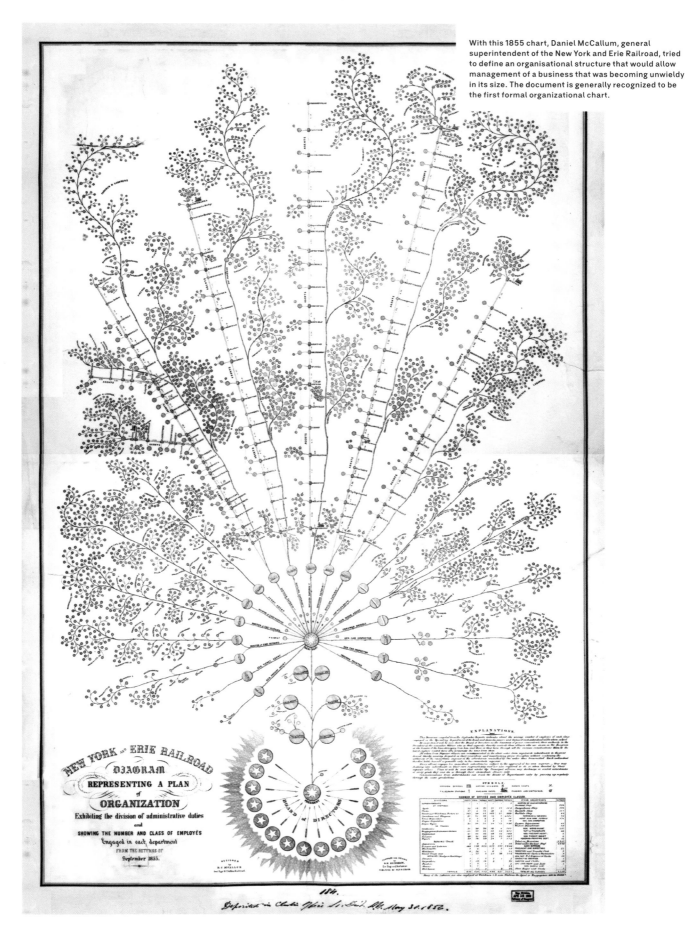

With this 1855 chart, Daniel McCallum, general superintendent of the New York and Erie Railroad, tried to define an organisational structure that would allow management of a business that was becoming unwieldy in its size. The document is generally recognized to be the first formal organizational chart.

Maps of time, process and flow

Interestingly, many family trees also contain an element of time: the process of family evolution, one could say. Though time is an element on these maps, the people and their connections are the most important data. There are specific types of maps where time and process takes center stage: timelines.

We have probably all either made or used a timeline at one point in our lives. Learning about history and understanding the order and consequence of events is easier (at least for many) when it is all visualised and simplified on a single page. The way that we visualise time is dependent on our conceptualisation of time, which has no doubt changed throughout history. Societies have also differed in the way that they imagine time, and while we now have a generally standardised way of dealing with time as a collective global society, there are some pockets who see time differently.

Most timelines are, as the name suggests, linear and events are plotted in chronological order. Historical timelines map a selection of what has been and gone.

Though timelines are not only reserved for historical events. Timelines of prospective events are now pervasive components of contemporary culture and one of the most valuable tools of any project manager. Timelines in the organisational management world can take many forms, though Gantt charts, flowcharts, and calendars are probably the most common.

In recent years, internet-connected sensors and enhanced GPS data have allowed for the tracking and observation of the process and flow of various entities in real time. From road traffic to web traffic, the tracking of e-waste around the world and migration patterns of endangered species, these real-time maps of journeys and flow give their readers deep insight into patterns of movement, and more importantly, the forces and factors that influence them. These maps have the power to change minds, regulations, and policies.

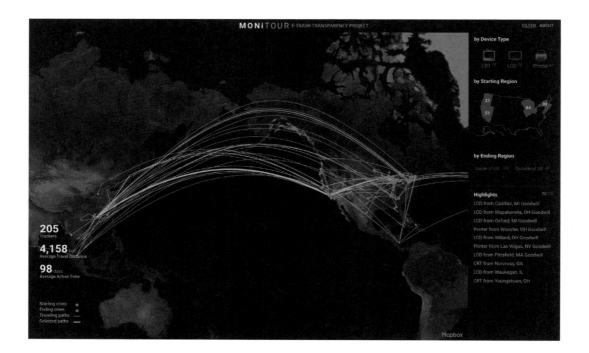

Above: A screenshot of an interactive map produced by MIT's Senseable City Lab visualizing exports of e-waste.

Opposite top: A New Chart of History published in 1769 by 18th-century British polymath Joseph Priestley. This chart was unique in that it plotted the rise and fall of various empires, not just Western ones. Indeed, Priestley believed that the entire world's history was significant: "The capital use [of the Charts was as] a most excellent mechanical help to the knowledge of history, impressing the imagination indelibly with a just image of the rise, progress, extent, duration, and contemporary state of all the considerable empires that have ever existed in the world".

Opposite right: Charles Minard's famous Map of Napoleon's Russian Campaign of 1812 is a great example of a Flow Map — hybrids between maps and flowcharts where the movement of objects is mapped over time and space. More specifically, it is classified as a Sankey diagram, because the width of the arrows is proportional to the flow rate. While this is Minard's most famous map, it certainly isn't the only one he created. He mapped the flow of many things including coal, wine, people and languages. Minard believed maps should "speak to the eyes" and designed his maps to tell a story.

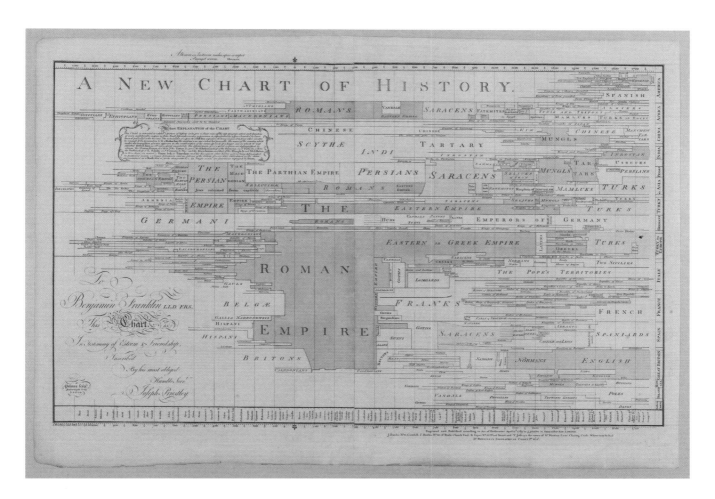

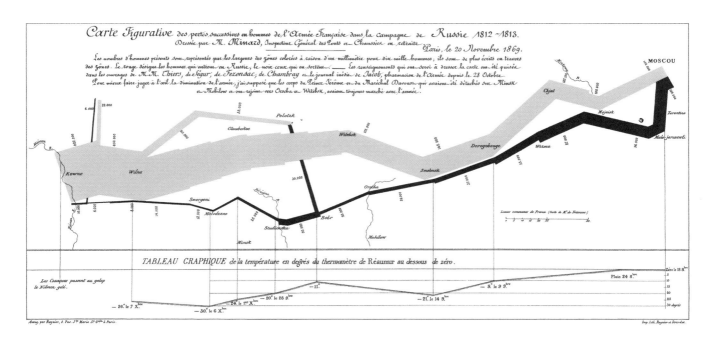

Maps of objects, machines and buildings

Engineers, designers, and architects communicate in very visual ways. They use an array of mapping methods to communicate early ideas for how things might function and look. They develop these into more concrete forms to instruct people or machines to construct their designs. These disciplines have developed very specific language to describe their mapping process, as their ideas move from the conceptual and prospective to the real and tangible. The maps that they make serve very different purposes along this journey. They also have very specific terms to describe the types of maps they make and the range of views and perspectives they use.

In architecture, as in many parallel design fields, maps or drawings are used for a number of purposes: to develop a design idea into a coherent proposal, to communicate ideas and concepts, to convince clients of the merits of a design, to assist a building contractor to construct it based on design intent, as a record of the design and planned development, or to make a record of a building that already exists.

Typically, architects, engineers, and designers use a set of conventions, which include particular views (floor plan, section etc.), sheet sizes, units of measurement and scales, annotation, and cross referencing. Various architectural and design drawings serve different purposes. Presentation drawings, for example, are intended to explain and promote the general idea of a design; they are not meant to be fully realistic and enable architectus to communicate the gist of the concept to various stakeholders.

Working drawings follow presentation drawings and guide a building construction project. These will include architect's drawings, in addition to structural and other engineering drawings in a larger set of drawings and documents. Before working drawings can be produced, architects typically commission survey drawings of existing land, structures and buildings, to establish the exact dimensions to work with.

Views are also really important in the realm of design and architecture. A floor plan is the most fundamental architectural diagram, a view from above showing the arrangement of spaces in a building in the same way as a map, but showing the arrangement at a particular level of a building. An elevation is a view of a building seen from one side, a flat representation of one façade. This is the most common view used to describe the external appearance of a building. A cross section, also simply called a section, represents a vertical plane cut through the object, in the same way as a floor plan is a horizontal section viewed from the top. Isometric and axonometric projections are a simple way of representing a three dimensional object, keeping the elements to scale and showing the relationship between several sides of the same object, so that the complexities of a shape can be clearly understood.

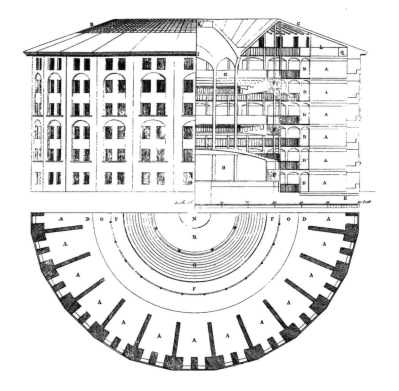

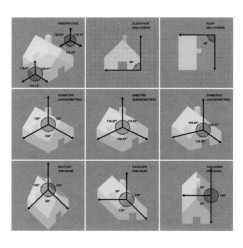

Above: Side-by-side comparison of types of graphical projection typically used in architecture and design.

Left: Architectural drawing combining elevation, section and plan: drawings by Willey Reveley of Jeremy Bentham's proposal for a Panopticon prison, 1791. Panopticon prison is a type of institutional building and a system of control. The design allows all prisoners of an institution to be unknowingly observed by a single security guard.

Maps of ideas, concepts and logic

Moving into the land of the abstract and intangible, we have maps of ideas, concepts and logic. Concept diagrams, mind maps, and semantic networks are all ways to organise and represent knowledge. They are common tools for brainstorming, note-taking, problem-solving, memory, learning, and visual thinking techniques used by psychologists, educators, engineers, and other professionals that need ways to structure and communicate the logic behind ideas, decisions, and frameworks.

In slightly different ways, these maps illustrate concepts and ideas, and the relationships among them. Mind maps tend to be more flexible ways of brainstorming, note-taking, visual thinking and communicating. They often start with one idea or question in the middle and branch from there. Although the distinction is blurry, concept maps tend to be more structured, connecting multiple large ideas through branches to indicate meaning and logic of ideas and how they are connected.

The Porphyrian Tree is commonly attributed as one of the oldest and most popular mind maps. It was created by philosopher Porphyry of Tyros as his understanding of one of Aristotle's great works, *Categories*. Based on his visual representations, he was able to better formulate his own ideas and communicate them in a way that could be easily understood by others.

The computer age has given rise to a more sophisticated type of mind map: the semantic network. Semantic networks help machines and humans process ideas and language quickly and efficiently. A semantic network illustrates the meaning of concepts through their relations to other concepts. Concepts are represented as nodes with labeled links (e.g., IS-A or Part-of) as relationships among the nodes. Thus, knowledge is a combination of information about concepts and how those concepts relate to each other[8].

Semantic networks have become increasingly important with the rise of Artificial Intelligence, and act as maps for computer decision making and reasoning processes. They can come in many forms based on their function, including but not limited to definitional, implicational and executable.

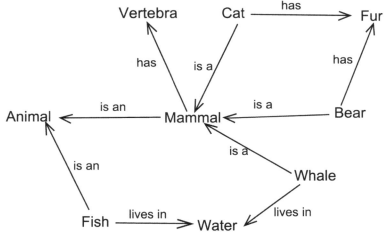

Top: The Tree of Porphyry as depicted by Franz Georg Hermann (1755–1757) in Bad Schussenried, Germany. The original Tree of Porphyry is the oldest known semantic network. It was drawn in the 3rd century AD by the Greek philosopher Porphyry in his commentary on Aristotle's categories.

Right: An example of a semantic network graph with 'Mammal' as the central node.

Maps of stories, the invisible, speculations, and utopia

We mostly think of maps as tools to help us navigate through space, time, and knowledge. What's more, they can help us understand how to build and construct things and make decisions. But maps can also transport us to other realms, highlight the invisible and prompt us to imagine fictional worlds or futures yet to manifest. Rather than influencing one's physical direction, these maps have the power to transport the mind, change beliefs, encourage further exploration and even start new movements.

Maps of utopia have historically been a common way to provoke alternative visions of the world, and continue to have influence today. Utopian maps have been particularly relevant in the connected fields of urban planning and political philosophy. Thomas Moore's 1516 *Utopia* is probably the most famous example, which depicts a fictional island society and its religious, social, and political customs. The extent to which Moore intended his work to represent "no place" or "the good place" is debated. Some see his imaginary society as a blueprint for an idealistic society, while others believe it is merely satirical, reflecting upon the England of his day. Regardless of its intent, his work and the maps that came alongside showed the power of mapping as a tool for extending reality and promoting critical reflection of the status quo.

There are other utopian maps that have inspired more concrete action and some have even inspired entire movements. Ebenezer Howard visualised his 'Garden City' concept in 1902 underpinned by ideas of social and urban reform. His encompassing work, *Garden Cities of Tomorrow* proposed that society be reorganised with networks of garden cities that would lead to a form of cooperative socialism in the perfect blend of city and nature[10]. His work and vision resulted in the 'Garden City Movement' and the actual building of various garden cities.

There is a distinct school of thought that acknowledges the role of maps in influencing and perpetuating power relations. Under the umbrella of critical cartography, the practices of counter-mapping, participatory and community mapping, and psychogeography go against traditional conceptualization of mapping as an objective and neutral reflection of the environment[11].

The term 'counter-mapping' was coined in 1995 to describe the commissioning of maps by forest users in Kalimantan, Indonesia, as a means of contesting state maps of forest areas that typically undermined indigenous interests[12]. The resultant counter-hegemonic maps had the ability to strengthen forest users' resource claims. The power of counter-maps to advocate policy change in a bottom-up manner led commentators to affirm that counter-mapping should be viewed as a tool of governance.

There are other related schools of thought that promote a dissident cartographic aesthetic and bottom-up approach to mapping. For example, the practice of Psychogeography was defined in 1955 by Guy Debord as "the study of the precise laws and specific effects of the geographical environment, consciously organized or not, on the emotions and behavior of individuals"[13].

From these perspectives, maps can be seen as personal or collective storytelling devices. In contrast to the perceived objectivity of official maps produced by centralised authorities in accordance with various standards, the point of these maps is to illustrate personal stories and map elements that often go unseen. They can do so purely for the sake of personal storytelling, or have a more activist motivating spirit.

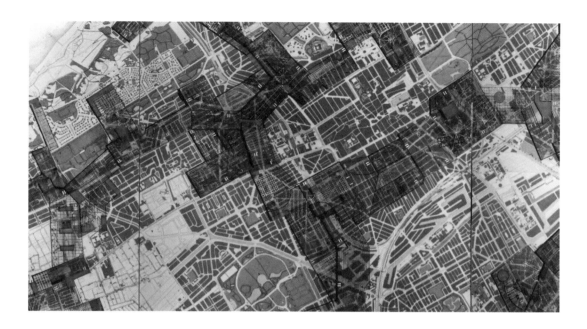

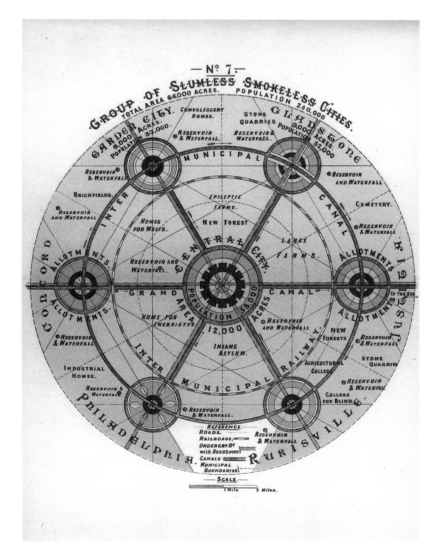

Opposite: Utopia as described by Thomas Moore, 1595, by Abraham Ortelius, a Flemish cartographer who is credited with producing the world's first modern atlas, *The Theatre of the World*[9].

Top: In 1956, Dutch artist Constant Nieuwenhuys (Amsterdam, 1920-2005) started work on a vast architectural and urban planning project that he called *New Babylon*. He worked on it non-stop for almost twenty years, expressing his ideas not only in architectural models, topographical maps, paintings, drawings and prints, but also in films, manifestos, texts and lectures. In 2004 he said, "New Babylon is not a model that should be imitated, but rather an illustration of a way of life in a hypothesized society."

Left: Howard's idealised garden city would house 32,000 people on a site of 6,000 acres (2,400 ha), planned on a concentric pattern with open spaces, public parks and six radial boulevards, 120 ft (37 m) wide, extending from the centre. The garden city would be self-sufficient and when it reached full population, another garden city would be developed nearby. In his 1902 book, *Garden Cities of To—Morrow*, Howard was careful to designate his city outline as a "diagram only" or "merely suggested."

Mapping as the language of polymaths

Rather than attributing maps and mapping to a single discipline or 'inventor', it is more productive to analyse maps and their makers as bridges between historical knowledge and new knowledge, and as translators across disciplines. Many maps notoriously combine and layer different types of knowledge to help wide audiences gain a shared understanding or view of a particular system, idea or vision. In many cases maps give their makers and users a new language to use to communicate to others. In fact, it has been argued that mapping is the language of polymaths, and many historical mapmakers have indeed been individuals known for drawing on complex bodies of knowledge to understand the world and solve specific problems. Maps, and the processes around them, have the ability to bring various strands of knowledge together and to bring diverse communities together, too. Importantly maps can also be exclusionary and divisive, and must always be read with constructive and critical eyes.

Some maps are made in isolation for the benefit of just the mapmaker or a closed community, other maps are made collaboratively for the use of collectives. Some maps are a means to an end, and other maps are the end in themselves. There is no single 'right' way to map and even those that claim to be the most objective and accurate have limitations. But while there is no single superior form of mapping, some maps work better in certain contexts than others. And it's worth learning, borrowing, and adapting techniques, formats, language, and values from other disciplines to enrich our own understanding and practice, and equip ourselves with more suitable mapping techniques and maps for contexts we know well, and those we have yet to explore.

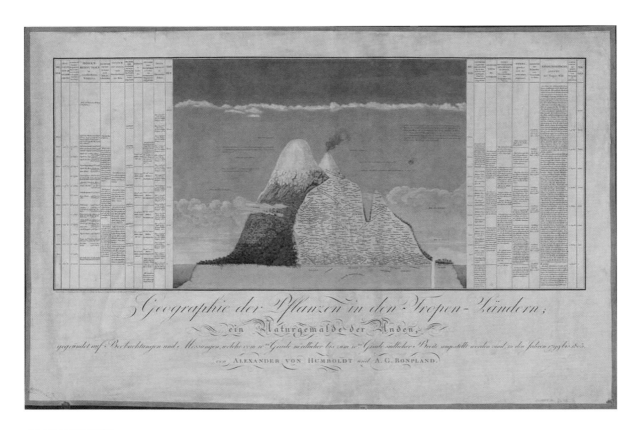

Top: Alexander von Humboldt (14 September 1769 – 6 May 1859) was a Prussian polymath, geographer, naturalist, explorer, and proponent of Romantic philosophy and science. He combined branches of knowledge to produce some of the greatest maps of his day. Humboldt's *Naturgemälde*, also known as the *Chimborazo Map*, is his depiction of the volcanoes Chimborazo and Cotopaxi in cross section, with detailed information about plant geography.

Left: Humboldt and his fellow scientist Aimé Bonpland near the foot of the Chimborazo volcano, painting by Friedrich Georg Weitsch (1810).

Florence Nightingale AN ANGEL OF MERCY. Scutari Hospital 1855.

Left: Florence Nightingale with her candle making the night round of the wards at Scutari hospital during the Crimean War. Coloured mezzotint, c. 1855, by Tomkins after Butterworth.

Below: Diagram dated 1858 by Florence Nightingale of a colored pie chart to illustrate causes of death in the British Army. Florence Nightingale was a pioneering polymath in establishing the importance of sanitation in hospitals through her work as a nurse in the Crimean War in the mid 1800s. She gathered data of death tolls and communicated this information through applied statistics and graphical communication. She is particularly famous for the development and use of certain graphs, now commonly known as coxcombs or polar area plots. These are graphical representations of spatio-temporal data.

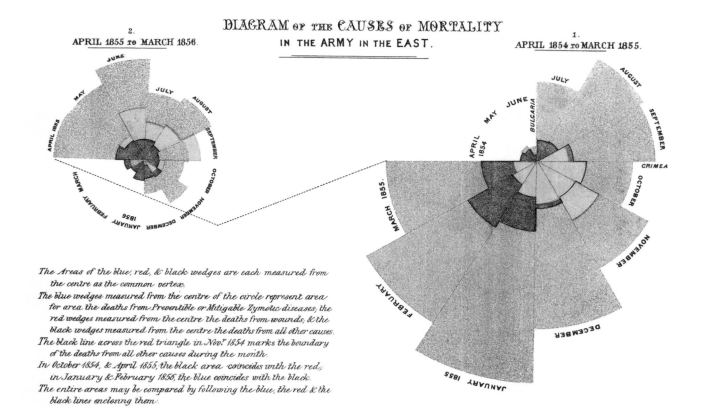

DIAGRAM OF THE CAUSES OF MORTALITY
IN THE ARMY IN THE EAST.

2.
APRIL 1855 TO MARCH 1856.

1.
APRIL 1854 TO MARCH 1855.

The Areas of the blue, red, & black wedges are each measured from the centre as the common vertex.

The blue wedges measured from the centre of the circle represent area for area the deaths from Preventible or Mitigable Zymotic diseases; the red wedges measured from the centre the deaths from wounds, & the black wedges measured from the centre the deaths from all other causes.

The black line across the red triangle in Nov.r 1854 marks the boundary of the deaths from all other causes during the month.

In October 1854, & April 1855, the black area coincides with the red; in January & February 1856, the blue coincides with the black.

The entire areas may be compared by following the blue, the red & the black lines enclosing them.

1 *Cambridge Dictionary*, Cambridge Dictionary, accessed 01 August 2020, https://dictionary.cambridge.org/dictionary/english/cartography

2 *Collins English Dictionary*, Collins Dictionary, accessed 01 August 2020, https://www.collinsdictionary.com/dictionary/english/uranography

3 "Types of Maps", PennState College of Earth and Mineral Science, Department of Geography, accessed 01 August 2020, https://www.e-education.psu.edu/geog486/node/641

4 Ibid.

5 "Mapping the body", Wellcome Collection, published 8 January 2018, https://wellcomecollection.org/articles/WjAAHyQAAEKPOuvC

6 Aaron Dignan, "The Org Chart Is Dead", published 27 February 2016, https://medium.com/the-ready/the-org-chart-is-dead-e1d76eca9ce0

7 Henry Mintzberg and Ludo Van der Heyden, "Organigraphs: Drawing How Companies Really Work", Harvard Business Review, (September–October Issue, 1999) https://hbr.org/1999/09/organigraphs-drawing-how-companies-really-work

8 Peter W. Foltz, "Semantic Processing: Statistical Approaches", *International Encyclopedia of the Social & Behavioral Sciences*, (2001), https://doi.org/10.1016/B0-08-043076-7/01547-3

9 Andrew Simoson, *The Size and Shape of Utopia*, accessed 01 August 2020, https://archive.bridgesmathart.org/2016/bridges2016-65.pdf

10 Robert Fishman, *Urban utopias in the twentieth century: Ebenezer Howard, Frank Lloyd Wright, and Le Corbusier* (Cambridge, Mass: MIT Press, 1982)

11 John B. Harley, *The new nature of maps: essays in the history of cartography* (Johns Hopkins University Press, 2001)

12 Nancy L. Peluso, "Whose Woods are These? Counter-Mapping Forest Territories in Kalimantan, Indonesia". *Antipode. 4*. No. 27 (1995): 383–406, doi:10.1111/j.1467-8330.1995.tb00286.x.

13 Guy Debord. *Introduction to a Critique of Urban Geography*. The Situationist International Text Library.

Project Global: Power

Learning from mapping in architecture

By Sanne van den Breemer (The Berlage)

Project Global forms part of the Berlage Post-Master in Architecture and Urban Design at the Delft University of Technology. As a research and design project it aims to explore design approaches with specific relevance to selected sites. This year's iteration, themed 'Power', forms part of a three year cycle that addresses the metabolism of cities. The ultimate goal is to reveal the niches where architecture is uniquely able to contribute to issues pertaining to urban resilience, or not.

65 lemmas, 13 maps, 6 mini atlases, and 13 architectural projects
Some hunches came up on the very first day, and never left the table. Throughout the different parts of the architectural research and design course/project, these ideas were supported with information, sharpened and solidified. Others developed gradually, in the course of the semester.

The selected sites were Paris and Tokyo. As an exemplar of the modern planned metropolis, Paris served as the starting point in examining urban systems, as a model city. Tokyo then formed the situation through which to interrogate this model, and the context for the architectural projects. These parts of the work coincided with three products: first a lexicon, second an atlas, and third a set of architectural projects.

In 65 lemmas, the lexicon was set up as an index for the course/project. The lemmas addressed diverse systems, ranging from various forms of power generation to many sectors of consumption, from current fields of innovation to well established techniques. They focused on related objects and institutions, systemic fragility and failure, the public opinion and its discrepancies, and the privileged image with which these systems are represented. The result was a list of notions that could be structured in various ways, illustrated with photographs, diagrams and found imagery.

The atlas related the systems of study to the specific geographic conditions of Tokyo, and the territorial entities it forms part of. Organised according to scale and phase of the energy cycle, the work started as a systematic exploration. In 13 maps, the relevance of each scale for each part of the cycle was considered. Six thematic mini atlases were then set up to further elaborate the spatial impact of the phases — raw materials, generation, transmission, distribution, consumption, and waste.

This formed a comprehensive base to start the architectural projects from. For some it led to an obvious next step, consistently developing an idea throughout the three phases. For others, the start of part three was a moment to decompose ideas, and recombine them. The 13 projects resulted in a varied range with respect to site, scale, and genre, each addressing different aspects of the energy cycle.

Beyond the frame of a set design brief, architectural research and design practice engages with multiple methods and techniques, for both analytical and projective purposes. In exploring a comprehensive topic — with the aim to

13 Maps
A set of maps relates the energy systems to the geographical conditions of Japan, considering how the systems are embedded within the territory at each scale. The thirteen defined scales range from the world, and the Japanese archipelago, to a typical Tokyo chōme and building block.

Selected maps:
Top: 'Gokaido' stands for the five centrally administered routes that connected Tokyo to its surroundings during the Edo period, covering the region from Kyoto in the West to Fukushima prefecture in the Northeast. Central to this area is the frequency frontier that divides between 50Hz electricity to the East and 60Hz to the West. At this scale, the frequency converter stations, and major transmission lines around Tokyo become apparent.

Middle: Centered around Tokyo Bay, the sixth map explores sites of power generation — from the hydro electricity power stations on the mountainous West side to the solar fields at the flat lands towards the East — as well as the import of fuel, and electricity generation along the bay.

Bottom: The scale of the twenty three Special Wards addresses the issue of waste. The dense urban area contains an expansive network of incineration plants, where the energy stored in materials is converted back to power, or reused in the form of heat.

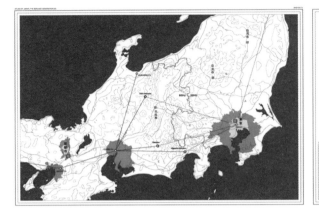

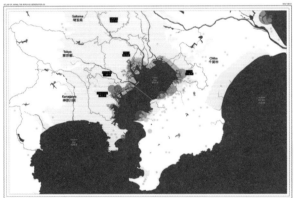

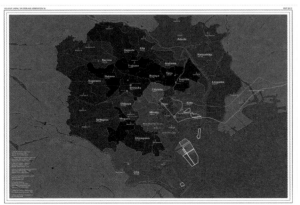

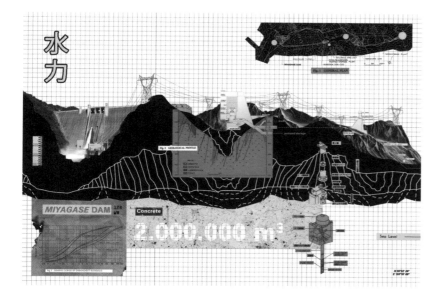

identify relevant design questions — this course/project made use of different methods to collect, select and structure information, and various formats to analyse and represent this. Cartography, architectural drawing, spatial diagramming, and combinations thereof, were all employed to start investigating systems, thereby always relating these to space, to grounds and to objects.

As addressed by Edward Tufte in the very first chapter of his seminal work *Envisioning Information*, to graphically represent the complexity and multidimensionality of the world, one needs to escape the 'flatland.' Tufte starts his didactic account with the example of a Japanese map of the famous Ise Shrine and its surroundings: a bird's-eye view depiction of the buildings, infrastructure and mountainous landscape, transitioning into a diagram representing the national railway system. A combination of scales and drawing projections positions an architectural complex within its local and national context, as part of a landscape and infrastructural network respectively. Beyond its significance as a local reference, this old map touches on aspects still relevant for our approach of the course.

Collage techniques offer another opportunity to relate different types of information and forms of representation. A key reference here is the work of James Corner in *Taking Measures Across the*

6 Mini Atlases
The thematic sections, or mini atlases, structure the energy cycle in six phases: raw materials, generation, transmission, distribution, consumption, and waste. For each phase, the miniatlases relate the systems to the ground, buildings and objects. Numbers and diagrams, commonly used to represent and communicate the themes of study, are used as a starting point to explore the spatial characteristics of the systems.

Top two: Sites of power generation are strongly linked to particular geographic conditions, from hydroelectric dams that operate on the premise of height difference, and thermal power plants that need cooling water in order to function, to wind turbines confined to the coast line, as they can't be transported over land due to their size. A cross section through the territory suggests the role of topography in relation to the systems — in reference to Patrick Geddes' *Valley Section*. Photographic imagery further links this to the (resulting) landscape.

Left: The waste to energy cycle, as well as its material remains, involves many structures and locations. Sites of collection, transportation, incineration, reuse, recycling, pulverization, and finally disposal all have a physical presence, embedded within the city.

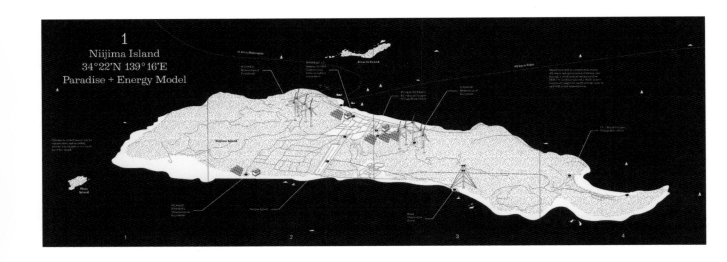

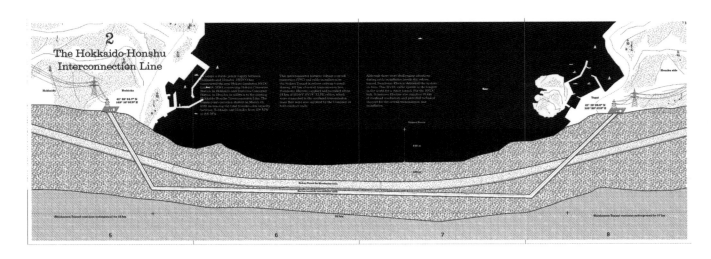

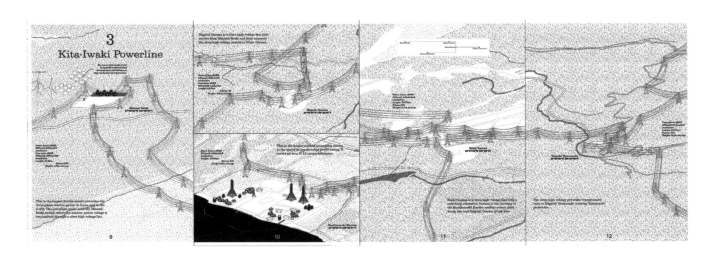

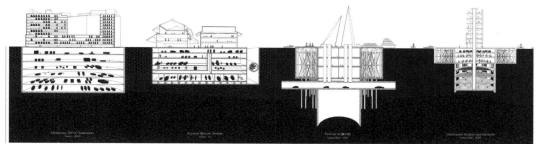

1
Half-buried

in the way these afford, invite, and oblige

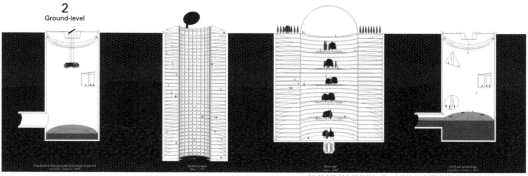

2
Ground-level

participation as 'design-by-doing' (Lim, 2008), while also permitting different

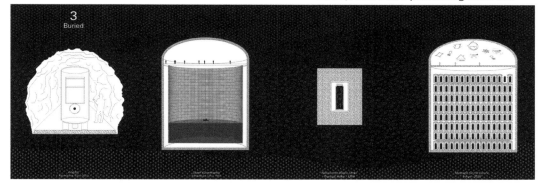

3
Buried

American Landscape. By combining fragments of maps, drawings, and photographic images, all extensively annotated, different landscape types, and the way these have been influenced by societies and technologies, are explored in the book. The giant structures facilitating power generation in the Japanese landscape have a complex relationship with their surroundings — for provision of input, absorbing of output, and ensuring physical stability. Collages allowed for a linking between engineering detail and topographical section, between process diagram and the resulting image in the landscape.

Besides the (obviously iterative) process of constructing the different maps and drawings — from the definition of the outline and drawing projection,

Opposite: A national grid of transmission lines connects sites of power generation to the vast amount of distribution networks, in order to ensure a stable supply of electricity. To cover the whole territory, many ambitious works of engineering have been realized. Test facilities on the isolated island of Niijima form a model for next developments.

13 Projects
The approaches to the architectural project are diverse, working with both singular sites and typical conditions, starting from systems, or objects, or grounds.

Selected material:
Above: 'Deep Underground' begins from a prototypical space: the underground building, mostly cylindrical in shape. Encountered as electrical substation, research facility, water storage facility, and utopian city, this building type is explored for the particular environmental conditions it generates, and the possible broader range of usage it could give space to.

to the selection of networks, sites, and objects to depict, to the set up of graphic styles — the process of constructing the project as a whole similarly went through various stages. The different drawings and maps produced for the atlas were crucial in analyzing and registering findings. The selection of found imagery, as part of the lexicon, furthermore contributed to the outlining of aspects of local culture. For the architectural projects, new drawing formats were set up and in cases experimented with, further specifying an investigation by means of a proposal.

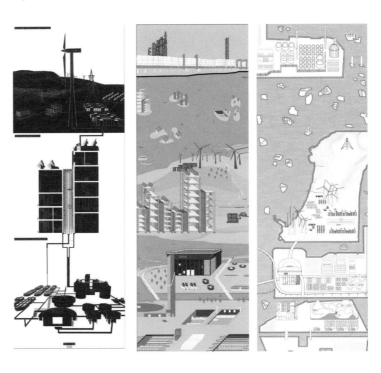

Top three: The project 'Muttso No Ruto: An Algae Archipelago' builds on existing systems, from the earthquake resilience gap, to waste water treatment facilities, to Niijima's experimental testing grounds. Integrating these with algae systems, a current focus on innovation, it aims at reaching a new environmental balance.

Right: 'Hinterlands of Power' takes its starting point in highly specific sites in which many forces are registered and of which the impact (potentially) far exceeds the local environment. The proposal for an electricity expressway identifies the potential to strengthen Japan's electricity network on the route from Tokyo (50Hz) to Shin-Shinano (50/60Hz), while making the new infrastructure part of the public experience.

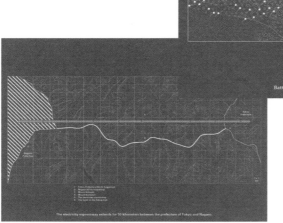

More project documentation can be found on the website
www.projectglobal.nl

Tutors: Filip Geerts and Sanne van den Breemer
Director of Studies: Salomon Frausto
Contributors: Santiago Ardila, Juan Benavides, Daniella Camarena, Stef Dingen, Marco Fusco, Jack Garay Arauzo, Theodora Gelali, Shaiwanti Gupta, Hao Hsu, Marianthi Papangelopoulou, Felipe Quintero, Gent Shehu, Siyuan Wang

Sanne van den Breemer is a graduate of the Berlage in Rotterdam. She also graduated cum laude from the Delft University of Technology, and has worked at several internationally oriented architecture offices. She has been teaching at the Berlage since 2013, and independently practices architecture and performs research projects in the Netherlands and abroad.

A system of systems

Learning from Systems Science and System Dynamics

By Megan Anderson (STBY) and
Brian Blankinship (Omplexity)

"The image of the world around us, which we carry in our head, is just a model. Nobody in his head imagines all the world, government or country. He has only selected concepts, and relationships between them, and uses those to represent the real system"

Jay Forrester, founder of System Dynamics

Service designers are increasingly addressing issues beyond the level of services, to the wider systems in which they are embedded. When it comes to systemic approaches and problem-solving, jargon feels rampant and it is easy to get confused and overwhelmed. There are blurry lines and multiple connections between 'systems science', 'system dynamics', 'systems thinking' and 'systemic design'. Though the epistemological foundations, approaches and tools of understanding systems may differ across these communities, they are all fundamentally concerned with higher order systems that encompass multiple subsystems.

The field of systemic design has emerged to integrate systems science and human-centered design, helping designers and design researchers approach complex, multi-stakeholder service systems and describe, map, propose, and reconfigure complex services and systems[1]. There is increasing awareness of the complementary nature of design research, service design and systemic design and they are connected in many ways . The tools and methods that systemic design[2] has integrated from systems science, and systems dynamics in particular, are worth exploring as they increasingly become part of our own language and repertoire.

A system of systems

There are of course multiple strands of academic and practitioner communities beyond the design community — falling mainly under the umbrella of systems science — concerned with systems-oriented approaches to complex problems in society, cognition, engineering, technology, and nature. From the perspective of systems scientists, the world is as a system of systems. The field has many different sub-disciplines worth exploring and learning from; this article focuses just on system dynamics.

System dynamics is a computer-aided approach to policy analysis and design, which aims to understand dynamic problems arising in a range of complex systems including social, managerial, economic, and ecological. System dynamics employs various techniques to frame, understand, and discuss complex issues and problems. Tools like causal-loop and stock-and-flow diagrams, and concepts like emergence, nestedness, and feedback help make sense of non-linear behaviour within complex systems.

System dynamics was originally developed in the 1950s by Jay Forester[3] and his colleagues at the Massachusetts Institute of Technology to help corporate managers improve their understanding of industrial processes. The field has since evolved to be used throughout the public and private sector for policy analysis and design. Pioneers like Donella Meadows helped apply system dynamics to broader societal issues like climate change in her seminal work on *The Limits to Growth*. Peter Senge popularised this way of thinking in the management world by conceptualising organisations as 'learning organisations': dynamic systems in states of continuous adaptation and improvement. While areas of application are diverse and expansive, the concepts and tools remain the same.

Project feature

System dynamics in action: Omplexity and the Taiwan COVID-19 strategy systems map

Developed by Omplexity, a Taiwan-based consultancy with expertise in systems mapping, this map shows the power of this approach in cultivating a "bigger picture" shared broadly among system stakeholders. That is no easy task when addressing complex adaptive challenges in dynamic systems. Omplexity's maps act as a gathering point for stakeholder dialogue and an impetus for coordinated action. For them, maps become useful when individuals who experience the system day-to-day can see themselves and their challenges in the map. Once the causal linkages are made explicit and can be seen, they can be understood, internalized, and challenged where need-be.

A causal loop diagram is principally about asserting a causal theory about the rules (or structure) of the system — a theory that can then be validated. That theory should describe why the system produces the results that it does. In this way, Omplexity uses systems maps both in a backward-looking way to make assertions about the structure of the system in the current reality, and in a forward-looking way, asserting a theory about how the system will look in the desired future state. They can also explore the dynamics in the transition from current reality to desired future.

Omplexity uses actor mapping alongside systems mapping. Actor maps are principally important because they acknowledge that no one

Legend
- ○ Stocks to Increase
- ◎ Stocks to Reduce
- ◉ Core Stocks to Reduce (Red Border)
- ● Intervention
- ● Barrier/Challenge
- ● Variable
- —— Positive Causality
- ······ Negative Causality

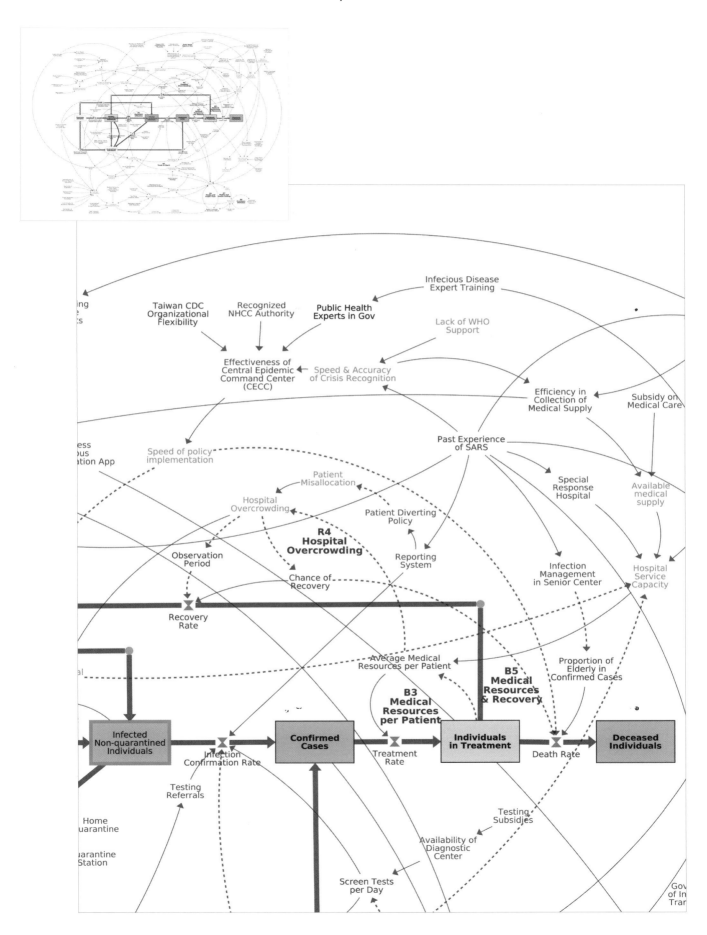

person can either: a) see the whole system, and b) change a system by themselves. Identifying those people is critical to aid in both the analysis of the system and the formation of a networked coalition. This coalition can use the systems map as the basis for developing, managing, and communicating their shared strategy to shift the system.

In reporting on Taiwan's odds-defying success in preventing community-level outbreak of COVID-19 in the first half of 2020, numerous media outlets had provided the international community with a strong case to study. While interesting, these reports had yet to establish a causal theory that described why Taiwan has been successful, something that was and still is desperately needed to make meaningful progress ahead of the next global threat.

The success of the policies discussed in this systems map are unique to the enabling conditions formed by Taiwan's governance, cultural norms, and societal memory. While no two countries sharing an identical strategy should expect similar results, Omplexity aimed to make Taiwan's context explicit in order to form some broadly applicable lessons for the international community.

To ensure that the strategy map is useful outside of Taiwan, Omplexity started their map by establishing a common framework, leveraging the Stock & Flow Diagram borrowed from the language of System Dynamics, to

track the potential number of people infected by and susceptible to infection with the novel coronavirus. Building on this framework, Omplexity then have assembled the many components that have made up Taiwan's context and collective response.

COVID-19 will not be the last shock we face as a global community. By contributing with this systems map, Omplexity does not offer a singular answer on what to do next, instead seeks to hold space for robust dialogue that will allow the world to accurately assess the state of our global health systems and establish a collective strategy that will lead to a future free from the threat of pandemic disease.

This map is produced and published by Omplexity and is published here with permission. To see the full interactive map, visit https://bit.ly/st7d9g7.

1 Jonas, Peter. "Systemic Design Principles for Complex Social Systems". in *Social Systems and Design, Gary Metcalf*, ed, Volume 1 of the Translational Systems Science Series, Springer Verlag, 2014.

2 Vink, Josina and Rodrigues, Vanessa. "What is the relationship between service design and systemic design?". Article December 2016 at Service Design for Innovation Network. http://servicedesignforinnovation.eu/what-is-the-relationship-between-service-design-and-systemic-desig/.

3 For further reading about Jay Forester and his work read: https://www.mckinsey.com/business-functions/strategy-and-corporate-finance/our-insights/the-beginning-of-system-dynamics#

Brian Blankinship is a systems mapper, facilitator, coach, and trainer at Omplexity where he works to empower systems leaders — those working to make positive impact beyond the bounds of their formal authority — and their stakeholders through participatory systems mapping. By allowing the individuals and organizations within a system to see themselves and one another as integral and interconnected, Omplexity's work raises collective capacity to handle complexity and enables transformational systems change.

A map is a map is a map

What geographical maps
and journey maps have
in common

By Michael Steingress
(More than Metrics)

Maps have been a key tool for people since the dawn of humankind. Starting from fading sketches drawn in sand to glowing Google Maps on screens, maps have always provided information, context, and orientation. They are one of our oldest ways to communicate, simplify, and share information. But maps can help us navigate more than the purely geographical. As defined by Harley and Woodward, "maps are graphic representations that facilitate a spatial understanding of things, concepts, conditions, processes or events in the human world"[1]. What helps us find our way through this world and understand various aspects of it, can also help us to understand our customers and businesses.

Visualising reality in 2D

Visualisations have two basic purposes: they help simplify complex contexts and they are the basis for further insights in analysis. Maps display spatial, temporal, and causal relationships. One of the main challenges in creating geographical maps is the complexity of the earth's surface that cannot be exactly represented on a map. Maps therefore are an approximation of reality only, and both mappers and readers of space and service journeys must take projection, scale, and generalisation into account.

A world map depicts the locations of different countries and also gives a good overview of the bigger picture, but it is not much help when navigating a specific city. On the other hand, a city map is not much help when travelling to another country. Scale is equally important in user journey maps. For one team, the interaction with a few touch points in granular detail might be most relevant, while for another it is more important to see and understand the entire flow more generally.

A lot of mapping is about simplifying complexity and communicating clearly. Selection of relevant information, and strategic use of symbology and design help mapmakers do this. Creators of maps, both geographical maps and journey maps, have to constantly ask themselves questions while mapping: "who is this map for and how will they use it? Which information is most important and what can I leave out? Is the map clear and easy to read?"

'Here be dragons': From assumption-based to data-backed maps

In times before satellites and drones, we had to explore the unknown step-by-step, mile-by-mile. The unknown has always been terrifying but some brave adventurers have always dared to go beyond the explored and fill the blank spots on the map.

In medieval times, unexplored territories have been illustrated by using dragons, monsters, and mythical creatures and the phrase 'Hic svnt Dracones' (Here be dragons) first appeared

Not every civilization sought to expand their territories, but many were drawn to exploring the unknown. For some, this meant going beyond the known borders of the world. For others, exploration meant gaining a deeper understanding of the details underlying the locally visible. Either way, curiosity led them to gather vast amounts of new information .

The very same idea could apply to organisations. Journey mapping helps them depict the known, discover knowledge gaps, and plan further research. What is the current normal might soon be outdated, and what seems to be true on a high-level perspective might not be so on a more granular scale. Parts of a customer journey (e.g. what customers are doing when not in direct interaction with a brand) are often a black box to organisations.

Assumptions are not questioned and maps are created that build the foundation of knowledge and action, but are not actually research-based. Just like the daring explorers of the past, researchers within organisations must venture beyond their 'known' world. And while assumptions are helpful in light of the unknown, mapping through research provides a way to fill knowledge gaps with data over time.

Maps help locate the unknown, define the limits of the known, plan where to start and go first, and to track where you've been. This applies to geographical maps in much the same way as it does to journey maps.

Important map elements

A map that does not contain metadata is difficult to use for navigation. You can hang it onto your apartment wall, but it will not serve you for much more than that. From a young age we learn how to read many maps, and some features and symbols become common sense over time. For example, we are used to reading topographic maps knowing that (most of the time) they display elevation using a specific colour range. Dark blue typically stands for deep sea, green for low elevation,, and red/ brown for high elevation of land masses.

Some elements — such as a legend, scale type, grids, northing, title, and author — are essential to every good navigational map. In the very same way, a journey map benefits from metadata as well. A legend, scale and scope, and structure (linear, columns, author, context) help to relate journey maps to a specific use case and are essential in making them boundary objects for different stakeholders.

The democratisation of mapping

The creation (and interpretation) of geographical maps have historically been based on specific technical and geographical bodies of knowledge that have only been available to a small group of experts. They have been of military, strategic, and economic importance for centuries. While the common man was not able to access or read maps for centuries, elites used maps to consolidate their power.

The same can be observed in organisations that are either highly hierarchical or that build strong silos. The ideal organisational culture and structure not only help to ease the gathering and sharing of information, but also promote the application of useful data to continuously improve an organisation's ability to compete in an increasingly customer-centric way. Journey maps function as guidelines and signposts in a troubled sea of constantly changing conditions. Which route to take, which sail to hoist, which cliffs to give a wide berth, and what is to be gained at the (sometimes unknown) destination are questions shared by both explorers of the past and strategists of the present.

In the same way that satellite-based remote sensing, the web 2.0, and low-cost GIS (geographic information system) democratised the creation, sharing, and availability of maps, user journey mapping software is opening up opportunities for service-orientated organisations. By listening to the voices of their customers, and proactively including them in the creation of new services, new mapping software is making organisational navigation more collaborative and transparent.

Top: A snippet of Carta marina et descriptio septentrionalium terrarum (Latin for Marine map and description of the Northern lands) created by Olaus Magnus and initially published in 1539. During medieval times, distant and unexplored lands on the edges of maps like this one were marked by drawings of dragons, sea serpents, and other ominous looking fictional animals.

Bottom: A 1755 map of Africa by the publisher M. Postlethwayt. It is a derivative of the 1749 map of Africa by the French cartographer Jean Baptiste Bourguignon d'Anville. D'Anville's notoriously left unknown areas of continents blank and noted doubtful information as such; compared to the lavish maps of his predecessors, his maps looked empty.

Above: Snippet of a user journey map from Smaply

Right: An example of a Topographic map legend.

The beauty, necessity, and power of maps

Visualisation builds on human capabilities to see patterns and helps to create mental images of complex matters. It offers a way to see the unseen, enriching the process of scientific discovery and fostering profound and unexpected insights[2]. In this way, maps are insightful and sometimes profound simplifications of complex phenomena. They can help to get an overview, but still uncover details and patterns. They help to illustrate spatial, temporal, and causal relationships . Good journeys maps, like effective geographical maps, deliver information in a precise and efficient way, and are always closely tied to clear objectives and communication goals.

On top of the mere power to provide information, contextualise it, and tailor it to an audience, maps also depend on a certain level of beauty. Beauty is what arouses our attention, sharpens our focus, and easily motivates us to return. A lot of maps also tell a story; the story of the undiscovered, a story that we've already experienced, or the story of which we are part of currently.

Maps help us to understand the world and business alike. In a complex environment and under constantly changing circumstances, maps give orientation, help us find our way back, open perspectives, and assist in understanding the world around us. What is true for understanding the world we are living in has many parallels with how we make sense of business and organisational landscapes.

Purpose and beauty make good maps. Good maps reveal a story. Stories are what help us understand the world. Understanding the world helps us change it for positive impact. And that's exactly what makes up the power of maps.

Michael Steingress studied tourism management and geography. As the Head of Partnerships and Sales at More than Metrics GmbH, he is in close contact with customers and business partners and knows what makes them tick. He helps them define their challenges and evaluate different approaches on how to tackle them with service design methods and tools. He also teaches at business schools and has a passion for maps of all kinds — not only journey maps.

1 J. Brian Harley and David Woodward (ed.), The History of Cartography (Chicago University Press, 1987), 3.

2 Bruce H. McCormick, Thomas A. DeFanti, and Maxine D. Brown, (ed), Visualization in Scientific Computing, Computer Graphics 21, No. 6 (November 1987), 3

On the ground

Learning from inclusive forms of mapping

By Constance Chung, Daphne Stylianou
and Megan Anderson (STBY)

Mapping, while seemingly objective, is fundamentally political and
a method of controlling a territory. It is not only used as a way to
visualise data and resources in a biased manner, it also acts as a tool
to manipulate the end result. 'Community mapping', 'counter mapping',
'ethnocartography' and 'cartopology' are typical mapping approaches
used in local communities as a way to democratise mapping. While
mapping has commonly been seen as a top-down practice, and maps as
artefacts from experts, these approaches are created in a participatory
and collective manner to empower individuals to participate in local
initiatives and advocate policy change. It is a process of creating
collective representations of geography and landscape in the community.
Moreover, these approaches also help local communities to better
understand their environment and give them power to control the use
of land and resources, protect local communities' rights and wellbeing.
With internet access on the rise and the support of geographic
information systems (GIS), individuals are able to manage and interpret
geographical data easily. Although these mapping practices all generally
involve a bottom-up, collaborative process, they have slightly different
traditions and use varying, yet interrelated methods.

Below: Imaging Homelessness in a City of Care was
a participatory mapping project undertaken with 30
single homeless people in Newcastle-upon-Tyne (UK) in
2014. The project's objectives were threefold: to pilot an
innovative mapping-based methodology; to offer single
homeless individuals an opportunity to comment on
local service provision and delivery; and to inform and
challenge public perceptions of homelessness
(detail of map).

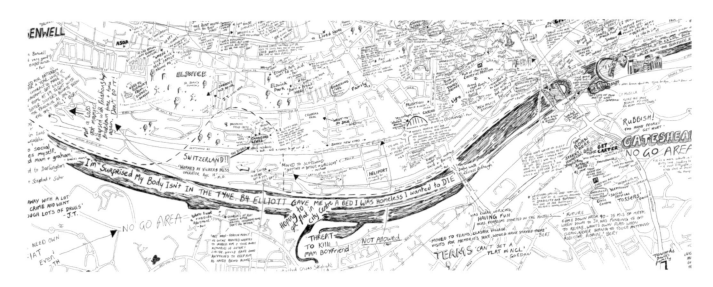

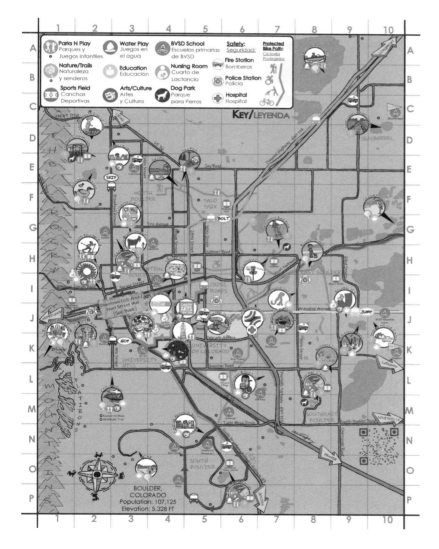

Community Mapping

The first community mapping in the UK was initiated by the charity Common Ground in 1985. They launched the Parish Map Project to encourage local people to map their own parished values in order to support local distinctiveness[1]. People were encouraged to employ any skills available to map their own place. The typical design comprises a bounded central map, surrounded by imagery relating to the place, events, or shared narratives. People used a diverse range of media to illustrate their place. This mapping approach grew in popularity toward the end of the 20th century.

Community mapping has now been used as a powerful spatial and planning tool for conducting citizen science, and connecting online and offline community engagement through mapping[2]. It is carried out and managed by communities with the intention of knowledge-sharing, local area protection, and social change. Data and thoughts are collected through a series of walking tours, video diaries, mapping parties and other engagements with the local community. In contrast to standardized forms of mapping, it empowers locals to be engaged in talking about local physical and social assets so as to identify the community capactiy and plan for future provision.

Counter Mapping

The term counter mapping was coined by the American rural sociologist Nancy Peluso in 1995[3]. It was originally used to describe the approach of indigenous people in Kalimantan, Indonesia who used conventional mapmaking techniques as a means to protect local claims to territory and challenge dominant power structures. It is a tool for indigenous identity-building, and for bolstering the legitimacy of customary resource claims. Mapping in official form enables comparison with the maps created by the authorities, which usually undermine indigenous interests. This approach has been most practiced in the developing world, but it is increasingly being applied by non-indigenous groups

Top: Participatory map of Yukpa territory, Toromo, Zulia, Venezuela. Community-based workshops bring together community representatives to work with cartographers and GIS specialists to represent histories, territorial boundaries, and material culture. With permission from Bjørn Sletto, University of Texas at Austin.

Bottom: Child-friendly city map of Boulder created by Growing Up Boulder in 2019 collaborating with 800 children and families, half of whom were from underrepresented populations. The map uses icons and it's written in English and Spanish to help families navigate nature trails, libraries, dog parks, and museums through the city. Public use.

in economically developed countries to fight against injustice in societies. As a cartographic tool, counter maps move away from a conventional view of the world towards revealing the experiences and knowledge of marginalised groups, minorities, and other vulnerable people where they may be otherwise overlooked.

The process that creates a counter map is the process of learning, living in, and knowing a place. The ties of place and identity are expressed in intangible values of shared experience and historical knowledge. While a conventional map may be disconnected from ownership and place-making, a counter map provides a different perspective by mapping elements like ancestral names and language, art, activities, myths, and traditions. Mapping the stories, memories, and cultural customs that build the identity of a place allows the mapmakers to express the meaning of a place and also contribute to public knowledge.

Ethnocartography

Ethnocartography[4] is a subdivision of traditional ethnogeography, a study of non-Western mapping practices. It refines the mapping methodology that enables maps not only to reveal practical data but also empirical data. The use of ethnocartography can be dated back to the 1920s. It was initially linked to cultural cartography of ethnic spaces, and it has been gradually used as a method in geographical and anthropological field research as a social cartography. It provides a way to study the social and cultural context of ethnic communities by examining land use and natural resources of indigenous communities[5] from their own memories, experiences and perspectives, so as to gain a deeper level of understanding of the use of space by traditional populations.

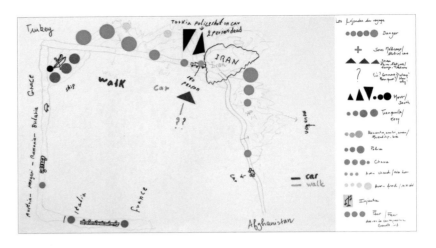

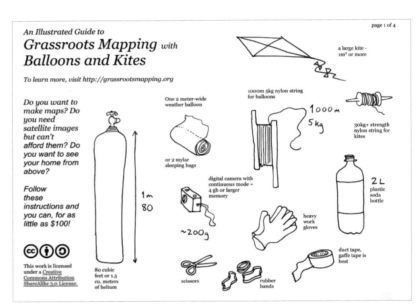

Top: The map presented here sketches a trail of exile from Afghanistan to France from the perspective of an asylum seeker. In order to read the map, it is necessary to read the map legend. Here the different symbols do not represent rivers or settlements; instead, they symbolise the fear, danger, police, injustice, friendship and love encountered enroute.

Bottom: Grassroots mapping with balloons and kites, in a refugee camp in Lebanon. This project set out to visualise water resources in the camp region. The initiative involved balloon mapping and a Do-It-Yourself (DIY) aerial photography tool to take aerial images from the camp and use them to produce a map of the refugee settlement.

Cartopology

The term 'Cartopology' was first coined by Dear Hunter and the Institute of Cartopology in 2018[6]. It is an interdisciplinary mapping approach that combines cartographic documentation techniques and anthropological observation skills with an artistic research practice[7]. Emphasizing the everyday life of a place and its spatial objects, it is a nonlinear way to visualise multi-layered pieces of information in the format of a map. The actual practice of cartopological research began in the sixteenth century when sea monsters were added to world maps to indicate unknown regions. Two centuries later Alexander von Humboldt began using maps to tell stories of the scientific data he collected. For him this was better than purely written, descriptive text in expressing interconnectedness of climate, geography, nature, and human societies[8]. Today, cartopology is now mainly used in policymaking for policy makers and designers to understand how the designed space is actually used. This kind of mapping can also be used as an artistic expression to reveal the stories of neglected places.

Top: Peoples of the Pacific map, by Miguel Covarrubias, 1940, Pacific House (Monterey, Calif.) The map illustrates the ethnic and racial groups in the Pacific region in 1940.

Bottom: This map was produced in the framework of the project 'Dear Landscape' and finally published in the 'Cartopological Landscape Sample Atlas of the Euregio Meuse-Rhine' (Dear Hunter, 2019). In Dear Landscape, six locations and their surroundings were mapped through intensive fieldwork. Local issues and insights were gathered: how do the different municipalities in this Three Countries Park deal with their landscape? How is it opened up? What are the distinctive qualities and how can they be used in a better way for the benefit of its inhabitants and/or its visitors?

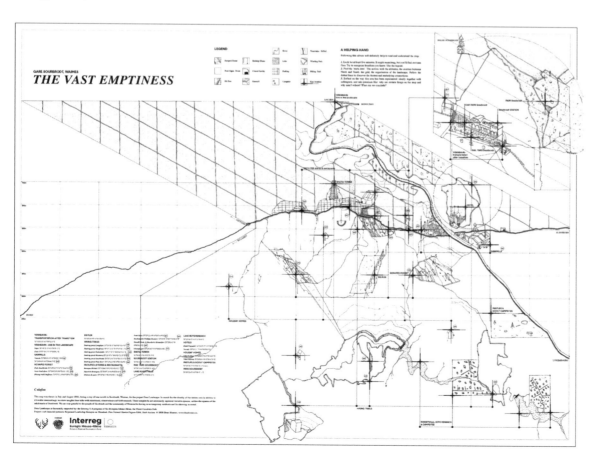

Constance Chung is a former STBY intern and graduate of the MA Service Design programme at the Royal College of Art. Having developed a deep connection with nature when she was a child in Hong Kong, most of her personal work is deeply influenced by the natural world and urges the audience to rethink their relationships with nature. She is interested in using design research as a method in developing service propositions that are good for both the societies and the environment.

Daphne Stylianou is a Design Researcher at STBY London. Working at the intersection of design and anthropology she investigates co-design methods for social innovation and sustainability. Her work is often collaborative, facilitating exchange between different disciplines. She has delivered talks and workshops on inclusive design for social challenges around themes of citizenship and democratisation of technology.

1 Angela King and Sue Clifford, *Holding Your Ground: An Action Guide to Local Conservation*, (Maurice Temple Smith, 1985).

2 Oxford Bibliographies. "Community Mapping". Accessed August 1 2020. https://www.oxfordbibliographies.com/view/document/obo-9780199874002/obo-9780199874002-0184.xml

3 Peluso, NL. "Whose Woods Are These? Counter-Mapping Forest Territories in Kalimantan, Indonesia, Antipode", 1995. Accessed August 1 2020. https://www.researchgate.net/publication/227846890_Whose_Woods_Are_These_Counter-Mapping_Forest_Territories_in_Kalimantan_Indonesia

4 Lovis, W. and Donahue, R. "Space, Information and Knowledge: Ethnocartography and North American Boreal Forest Hunter-Gatherers", 2011. Accessed August 1 2020. https://www.researchgate.net/publication/284454170_Space_Information_and_Knowledge_Ethnocartography_and_North_American_Boreal_Forest_Hunter-Gatherers

5 Dr. Araujo de Almeida, R. "Ethnocartography Applied To Environmental Issues", 2005. Accessed August 1 2020. http://www.cartesia.org/geodoc/icc2005/pdf/oral/TEMA10/Session%205/REGINA%20ARAUJO%20DE%20ALMEIDA.pdf

6 Institute of Cartopology. "A Home for Border Crossers". Accessed August 4 2020. https://instituteofcartopology.tumblr.com/framing

7 Dear Hunter. "Mapping Scene". Accessed August 4 2020. https://dearhunter.eu/mappingscene/

8 Miller, G. "The Pioneering Maps of Alexander von Humboldt". Smithsonian. Accessed August 4 2020. https://www.smithsonianmag.com/history/pioneering-maps-alexander-von-humboldt-180973342/

Tell me a story

On the deceptions of maps, 'soft mapping' and 'painterliness'

By Megan Anderson (STBY) and Dorota Gazy (STBY)

"To ask for a map is to say 'tell me a story'"

Peter Turchi, *Maps of the Imagination: The Writer as Cartographer*

Maps in the service design field tend to have a rather clean, graphic, and minimal visual style. They often use vector lines and illustrations, pictograms, and internationally recognised symbols and signs. This somewhat more neutral language makes maps, which are often very complex, easier to read and understand for a larger audience. It helps to align different users and establish a shared language among them. Such a clean visual language also creates a sense of impartialness, giving the impression of the map as an objective analysis of the area of inquiry. Like all design artefacts though, maps are made from a particular perspective and are underpinned by a particular understanding of the world. While seemingly ordered and 'objective', such an aesthetic may hide crucial biases and prevent critical dialogue around the lived experiences of the system in question.

Unpacking stylistic choices

There are various mapping communities that celebrate a more explicitly critical or subjective approach to mapping, and this is often reflected in the aesthetics of the maps that they make. Critical and ethno-cartographic approaches are a lot more artistic and experimental with spatial representation and style. Local communities often use mapping as a tool to counter hegemonic and scientific conceptualisations of the places they inhabit or interact with.

For them, the main purpose of a map is to tell a personal story, share an experience or counter a commonly held narrative. There is often visible emotion and anecdotal annotation included on these maps, favouring personal expression over graphical and scientific precision. Of course, this is not all black and white, and maps can sit along a spectrum. There are beautiful examples of maps that combine approaches or sit somewhere in between the extremes of scientific and artistic.

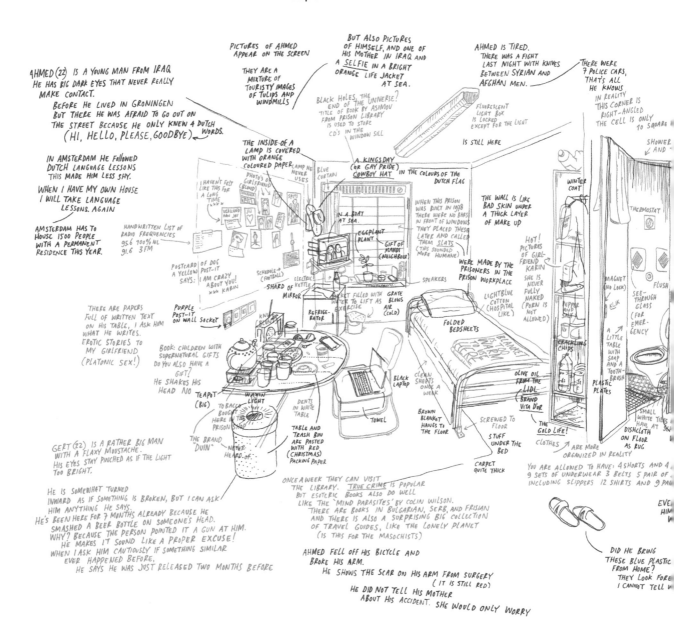

AHMED (22) IS A YOUNG MAN FROM IRAQ
HE HAS BIG DARK EYES THAT NEVER REALLY
MAKE CONTACT.
BEFORE HE LIVED IN GRONINGEN
BUT THERE HE WAS AFRAID TO GO OUT ON
THE STREET BECAUSE HE ONLY KNEW 4 DUTCH
(HI, HELLO, PLEASE, GOODBYE) WORDS.

IN AMSTERDAM HE FOLLOWED
DUTCH LANGUAGE LESSONS
THIS MADE HIM LESS SHY.

WHEN I HAVE MY OWN HOUSE
I WILL TAKE LANGUAGE
LESSONS. AGAIN

AMSTERDAM HAS TO
HOUSE 1500 PEOPLE
WITH A PERMANENT
RESIDENCE THIS YEAR.

PICTURES OF AHMED
APPEAR ON THE SCREEN

THEY ARE A
MIXTURE OF
TOURISTY IMAGES
OF TULIPS AND
WINDMILLS

BUT ALSO PICTURES
OF HIMSELF, AND ONE OF
HIS MOTHER IN IRAQ AND
A SELFIE IN A BRIGHT
ORANGE LIFE JACKET
AT SEA.

AHMED IS TIRED.
THERE WAS A FIGHT
LAST NIGHT WITH KNIVES
BETWEEN SYRIAN AND
AFGHAN MEN.

THERE WERE
7 POLICE CARS,
THAT'S ALL
HE KNOWS
IN REALITY
THIS CORNER IS
RIGHT-ANGLED
THE CELL IS ONLY
10 SQUARE

SHOWER
AND

BLACK HOLES, THE
END OF THE UNIVERSE?
TITLE OF BOOK BY ASIMOV
FROM PRISON LIBRARY
IS USED TO STORE
CD'S IN THE
WINDOW SILL

FLUORESCENT
LIGHT BOX
IS LOCKED
EXCEPT FOR THE LIGHT

IS STILL HERE

THE INSIDE OF A
LAMP IS COVERED
WITH ORANGE
COLOURED PAPER

LAMP HE
NEVER
USES

BLUE
CURTAIN

A KINGSDAY
(OR GAY PRIDE)
COWBOY HAT

IN THE COLOURS OF THE
DUTCH FLAG

WINTER
COAT

THERMOSTAT

I HAVEN'T FELT
LIKE THIS FOR
A LONG
TIME

PHOTO'S
OF GIRLFRIEND
(BLOND)

SPICE

IN A BOAT
AT SEA

EGGPLANT
PLANT

GIFT OF
MARDI
(NEIGHBOUR)

WHEN THIS PRISON
WAS BUILT IN 1978
THERE WERE NO BARS
IN FRONT OF WINDOWS
THEY PLACED THESE
LATER AND CALLED
THEM SLATS
(THIS SOUNDED
MORE HUMANE)

THE WALL IS LIKE
BAD SKIN UNDER
A THICK LAYER
OF MAKE UP

HOT!
PICTURES
OF GIRL-
FRIEND
KARIN
SHE IS
NEVER
FULLY
NAKED
(PORN IS
NOT
ALLOWED)

HANDWRITTEN LIST OF
RADIO FREQUENCIES
95.6 100% NL
91.6 3FM

POSTCARD OF DOG
A YELLOW
POST-IT
SAYS: I AM CRAZY
ABOUT YOU!
xxx KARIN

SCHEDULE
(FOOTBALL)

SHARD OF
MIRROR

ELECTRIC
KETTLE

SPEAKERS

WERE MADE BY THE
PRISONERS IN THE
PRISON WORKPLACE

LIGHTBLUE
COTTON
(HOSPITAL
LIKE)

MAGNET
(NO LOCK)

FLUSH

SEE-
THROUGH
GLASS
(FOR
EMER-
GENCY)

KLIK

A
LITTLE
TABLE
WITH
SOAP
AND A
TOOTH-
BRUSH

PEPPER
SALT

THERE ARE PAPERS
FULL OF WRITTEN TEXT
ON HIS TABLE, I ASK HIM
WHAT HE WRITES.
EROTIC STORIES TO
MY GIRLFRIEND
(PLATONIC SEX!)

PURPLE
POST-IT
ON WALL SOCKET

BUCKET FILLED WITH GRATE
WATER TO LIFT AS
(EXERCISE) BLOWS
AIR
(COLD)

REFRIGE-
RATOR

KNIFE

FOLDED
BEDSHEETS

CRACKLING
CHIPS

PLASTIC
PLATES

BOOK: CHILDREN WITH
SUPERNATURAL GIFTS
DO YOU ALSO HAVE A
GIFT?
HE SHAKES HIS
HEAD NO

TEAPOT
(BIG)

WARM
LIGHT

TOBACCO
BOUGHT
HERE IN THE
PRISON SHOP

DENTS
IN WHITE
TABLE

BLACK
LAPTOP

TOWEL

CLEAN
SHEETS
ONCE A
WEEK

OLIVE OIL
FROM THE
LIDL
BRAND
VITA D'OR

THE
GOLD LIFE!

SMALL
WHITE TILES
HAVE AT SE
DISHCLOTH
ON FLOOR
AS RUG

GERT (22) IS A RATHER BIG MAN
WITH A FLAXY MOUSTACHE.
HIS EYES STAY PINCHED AS IF THE LIGHT
TOO BRIGHT.

HE IS SOMEWHAT TURNED
INWARD AS IF SOMETHING IS BROKEN, BUT I CAN ASK
HIM ANYTHING HE SAYS.
HE'S BEEN HERE FOR 7 MONTHS ALREADY BECAUSE HE
SMASHED A BEER BOTTLE ON SOMEONE'S HEAD.
WHY? BECAUSE THE PERSON POINTED IT A GUN AT HIM.
HE MAKES IT SOUND LIKE A PROPER EXCUSE!
WHEN I ASK HIM CAUTIOUSLY IF SOMETHING SIMILAR
EVER HAPPENED BEFORE,
HE SAYS HE WAS JUST RELEASED TWO MONTHS BEFORE

THE BRAND
'DUIN'

NEVER
HEARD OF.

TABLE AND
TRASH BIN
ARE PASTED
WITH RED
(CHRISTMAS)
PACKING PAPER

BROWN
BLANKET
HANGS TO
THE FLOOR

SCREWED
TO
FLOOR

STUFF
UNDER THE
BED

CLOTHES

ARE MORE
ORGANIZED IN REALITY

CARPET
QUITE THICK

ONCE A WEEK THEY CAN VISIT
THE LIBRARY. TRUE CRIME IS POPULAR
BUT ESOTERIC BOOKS ALSO DO WELL
LIKE THE 'MIND PARASITES' BY COLIN WILSON.
THERE ARE BOOKS IN BULGARIAN, SERB, AND FRISIAN
AND THERE IS ALSO A SURPRISING BIG COLLECTION
OF TRAVEL GUIDES, LIKE THE LONELY PLANET
(IS THIS FOR THE MASOCHISTS)

AHMED FELL OFF HIS BICYCLE AND
BROKE HIS ARM.
HE SHOWS THE SCAR ON HIS ARM FROM SURGERY
(IT IS STILL RED)
HE DID NOT TELL HIS MOTHER
ABOUT HIS ACCIDENT. SHE WOULD ONLY WORRY

YOU ARE ALLOWED TO HAVE: 4 SHORTS AND 4
9 SETS OF UNDERWEAR 3 BELTS 5 PAIR OF
INCLUDING SLIPPERS 12 SHIRTS AND 9 PAN

DID HE BRING
THESE BLUE PLASTIC
FROM HOME?
THEY LOOK FORE
I CANNOT TELL W

EVE
HIM
W

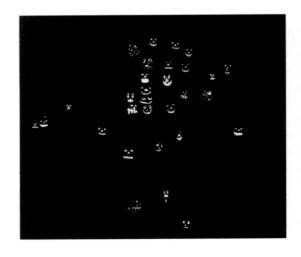

Top: Dutch visual artist Jan Rothuizen developed the
term 'Soft Maps' to refer to maps with information that
is subjective. Soft maps represent a unique form of
topographical journalism that document and visualise
his personal experiences and observations of urban
life. This drawing maps a cell in the Bijlmer prison in
Amsterdam, in blue, that was later turned into an asylum
seekers home, in red. The artist visited the same cell
twice, once when it was a prison, and later again when it
was a home for asylum seekers. Some things were still
the same, others were not.

DE MEESTE DROMEN ZIJN BEDROG

(handwritten note annotations around the drawing:)

E MAKES
HOME
METHING
E ARABIC MUSIC.
S.

SMOKE ALARM (NEW?)

INTERCOM AND ALARM BUTTON

(MOST DREAMS ARE DECEIVING!)

FAMOUS DUTCH SONG

SOUNDS LOUD FROM ONE OF THE CELLS.

THIS IS THE ROOM OF MAHDI, A BALDING MAN OF 47 FROM IRAN, HE IS LIKE A FATHER FOR AHMED. HE TELLS ME HIMSELF LAST WEEK HIS RESIDENCE APPLICATION WAS DENIED AND HE HAS TO LEAVE THE NETHERLANDS. I TELL HIM I'M SORRY FOR HIM BUT HE SMILES AND SAYS: 'I LIVE TODAY'

RESHENER
LET
ES ARE
ON YELLOW
NG WIDES

IT SMELLS LIKE A PRISON HERE (ANIMAL LIKE)

GEL WITH ECTRO FORCE MBS, 1 BRUSH 2 SHAVERS

OFFICIALLY THERE ARE 5000 DISMISSED ASYLUM SEEKERS LIVING IN THE NETHERLANDS

IN AMSTERDAM ABOUT 500 DISMISSED ASYLUM SEEKERS MAKE USE OF THE VERY SOBER BED-BATH-BREAD-SHELTER

I WAS HERE (AGAIN) ON JUNE THE 2ND 2017 FROM 9.45 TILL 10.50 IN THE MORNING

THE UNHCR ESTIMATES THERE ARE 10.000

TODAY IS 21ST OF SEPTEMBER 2009 10:25

THIS CELL IS ON THE 9TH FLOOR IN 'DE WEG' A TOWER WITH REPEAT OFFENDERS.

THE PRISON CLOSED IN 2016 AND REOPENED 2 MONTHS LATER AS AN ASYLUM CENTRE WITH HOUSING FOR 7000 PEOPLE. CURRENTLY 600 PEOPLE LIVE HERE.

ZANNE SENDS
EARN THROUGH

THE 'BIJLMERBAJES' HAS 6 TOWERS. EACH TOWER CONSISTS OF 5 PAVILIONS WITH 24 CELLS, A FEW OF THESE ARE FOR MORE THAN ONE PERSON. THE PEOPLE IN THIS PRISON HAVE NOT YET BEEN CONVICTED

SENT HIM THE DUTCH WORD FOR: NT'
AHMED READS IT OUT LOUD WITHOUT UNDERSTANDING AND LOOKS AT ME WITH BIG QUESTION MARKS IN HIS EYES

Learnings from fine art

A discussion on the aesthetics and purpose of maps can be enhanced by the concept of 'painterliness', borrowed from the art world. Based on the German term *malerisch*, the word refers to the opposite of 'linear' or 'plastic' design. A painting is 'painterly' when there are visible brushstrokes without closely following carefully drawn lines. In this way, painterly techniques can be considered expressionist, presenting the world from a subjective perspective and distorting it radically for emotional effect. Unlike more linear works, painterly styles seek to evoke moods rather than capture a physical reality through the use of the many visual effects produced by paint on canvas such as chromatic progression, warm and cool tones, complementary and contrasting colours, broken tones, broad brushstrokes, sketchiness, and impasto.

In much the same way as the artists in these movements, mappers who adopt a more subjective approach use different techniques to serve their motivations. Ethno-cartographic and counter-maps will sometimes appear more like pieces of art: painted or drawn, instead of digitally produced. Computed scale and accurate perspective are often not prioritised. Instead, views are skewed to depict the experiences, feelings, and perceptions of the mapmakers. Legends do not contain standard universally-accepted symbols, but use unique symbols that depict and communicate personal emotions, sensations or places of significance. For them, the objective of the map is not necessarily to show people the way, but rather to tell people a story.

Opposite: This map, called *jack-o-lantern*, is featured in the book *Everything Sings: Maps for a Narrative Atlas* by Denis Wood. Its caption reads: "I rode through the neighbourhood on my bicycle — it was 1982 — and took pictures of all the jack-o'-lanterns. On the map, there's a jack-o'-lantern at every address where there was one or more pumpkins on the porch..." It sits alongside numerous other intriguing maps of Boylan Heights, a single neighbourhood in Raleigh, North Carolina. Ira Glass, the author of the books' introduction, describes the maps as follows: "These maps are completely unnecessary. The world didn't ask for them. They aid no navigation or civic-minded purpose. They're just for pleasure...

Left: Portrait of Baronne de Rothschild (1848), Rothschild Collection, Paris by Jean-Auguste-Dominique Ingres in a more linear style.

Right: Portrait of Jeanne Samary, 1877, Pushkin Museum, Moscow by French impressionist painter Pierre-Auguste Renoir exemplifies a painterly style. The Impressionists, Fauvists and the Abstract Expressionists tended strongly to be painterly movements.

'Reading' a map

There is, of course, no single 'right' way to map, and mappers will typically choose their approach and style based on their intent. Importantly though, all maps have some sort of inherent bias, and bias is not necessarily bad. Bias can be celebrated for highlighting a particular perspective clearly. At the same time, bias can also do harm, by perpetuating stereotypes and reinforcing unjust power structures. When bias is hidden behind a guise of scientific language and symbology, and fails to acknowledge other perspectives, it may become dangerous. It is therefore important that we learn to read all maps and mapping processes, both 'soft' and 'hard', with a critical eye.

The practice of critical cartography aims to reveal the hidden agendas of cartography as tools of socio-spatial power. The critical cartographer sees the process of mapping as iterative steps of encoding and decoding. Translation and abstraction facilitate encoding and decoding as the mapmaker moves back and forth between concrete observations and conceptual ideas or models. While encoding and decoding maps, critical cartographers question their orientation, translation, organisation, and dimension. In this way we can reflect upon how maps actively shape our understanding of the physical, political, and social world, and how those understandings, in turn, influence the makers of maps, the tellers of stories, and painters of portraits.

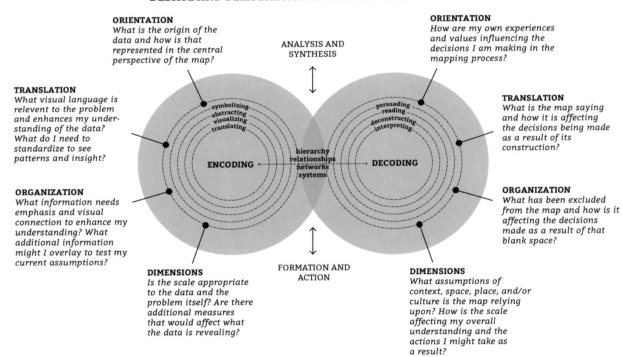

DEBATE AND DELIBERATION IN CRITICAL CARTOGRAPHY

ORIENTATION
What is the origin of the data and how is that represented in the central perspective of the map?

ANALYSIS AND SYNTHESIS

ORIENTATION
How are my own experiences and values influencing the decisions I am making in the mapping process?

TRANSLATION
What visual language is relevent to the problem and enhances my understanding of the data? What do I need to standardize to see patterns and insight?

TRANSLATION
What is the map saying and how it is affecting the decisions being made as a result of its construction?

symbolizing
abstracting
visualizing
translating

persuading
reading
deconstructing
interpreting

hierarchy
relationships
networks
systems

ENCODING

DECODING

ORGANIZATION
What information needs emphasis and visual connection to enhance my understanding? What additional information might I overlay to test my current assumptions?

ORGANIZATION
What has been excluded from the map and how is it affecting the decisions made as a result of that blank space?

DIMENSIONS
Is the scale appropriate to the data and the problem itself? Are there additional measures that would affect what the data is revealing?

FORMATION AND ACTION

DIMENSIONS
What assumptions of context, space, place, and/or culture is the map relying upon? How is the scale affecting my overall understanding and the actions I might take as a result?

This framework, developed by Allen and Queen (2015), helps us move beyond the examination of the artifact (i.e. the map) to include the critical evaluation of the activity of map making itself. Central to critical cartography is provoking debate and deliberation throughout the process of encoding and decoding.

Dorota Gazy is a design researcher at STBY. She is a graduate of Design Academy Eindhoven. Prior to the Design Academy she completed a Bachelor and Master degree Art History at the University of Amsterdam and VU University Amsterdam. As a researcher she seeks hidden patterns and moments where we take things for granted in order to design concepts that raise questions and trigger action.

New Territories

STBY in conversation with Dr. Kate McLean

Sensory Mapping

Through mapping smells, Dr. Kate McLean makes the invisible, visible. She leads international public 'smellwalks' and translates the resulting data using digital design, watercolour, animation, scent diffusion and sculpture into smellscape mappings. In 2019 she completed her PhD, "Nose-first: practices of smell walking and smellscape mapping" at the Royal College of Art. We sat down with her to discover more about her intriguing process, her stunning maps, and what it means to follow one's nose. This is a condensed version of our conversation.

A lot of famous mappers are referred to as 'polymaths' because they draw on so many different disciplines. Can you relate at all to this?

In order to be able to understand the idea of the smellscape, you do have to grasp the fundamentals of physiology, biology and chemistry, to understand how the sense of smell works, and a little physics and meteorology to comprehend the optimal conditions for humans to be able to smell.

A 'smell' doesn't exist until we name it. The odour molecules that we sense are not actual smells until we perceive them. Odour molecules in the air are trapped in the human nose by cilia in the olfactory epithelium and pass into odour receptor cells where information about the molecules is subsequently transmitted to the olfactory bulb in the brain. This becomes really interesting when you return to the concept of odour molecules in the air and start to visualize them as lightweight, floating objects subject to the vagaries of wind, eddies and temperature. This is where some rudimentary imaginings of Brownian motion and meteorology enable me to understand possible dispersal models for 'smells' in the air.

I am especially interested in human perception of smellscapes which is where my practice-based research is situated. I interpret and visualize smells that belong to the people who live in the cities I am mapping. Only they know what the smells are, and where they might come from. When I am working on a project I research the cartographic history and contemporary visual cartographic languages so as to translate the smells into something that people will understand at a local level. My work is very much done for a local population who will understand where specific locations might be and will relate to the smellscape map of their city.

You have an unique set of data gathering methods, like 'smell walks', 'smell catching' and 'smell hunting'. Can you tell us a bit more about these?

To start, the smell walk is simply a wonderful event! At the start of every smell walk I provide participants with 'smell notes' where they write the name of the smells they encounter, as well as the smells' intensity and duration. Both qualitative measures play an important part in the mapping. Sometimes smell walk participants also add the hedonic tone of a smell and the relative expectation of the olfactory encounter. When it comes to naming smells, both literal and lyrical names work equally well; 'the smell of shattered dreams' is probably the most lyrical name that I've ever come across. It refers to the smell of stale beer on the sidewalk. But 'the shattered dreams' smell comes with contextual information from the smell walker. She explained, "I'm 18 years old,

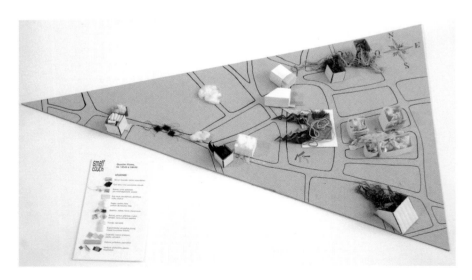

Smellscape Mapping in Marseille: For 4 days in February 2015 12 groups of design students smellwalked 12 separate pre-allocated 30 degree geometric sectors, sniffing, seeking and recording.

In their groups of 4 they created performative, experiential 'mappings' of the olfactory spaces of their findings.

I've left the bar, it's nine o'clock at night and I'm on my own again".

During smell walks, participants start with a smell catching exercise, which is where you breathe normally and inhale deeply when you detect a smell. It enables them to focus on the practice of smelling and the 'sniff' increases the smell molecules' chances of reaching the olfactory epithelium. The second stage is called smell hunting, in which participants deliberately deploy other senses to seek potential sources of interesting smells. They might use their ears to hear a truck with its engine running, or see an incredibly vibrant flower and that looks like it should smell delicious, or crush a leaf to release its fragrance.

The third, and final, section of the smell walk is a mini independent research project where participants smell four examples of a single object; bicycles, benches, leaves in order to develop a diversified olfactory vocabulary in place of the descriptors we use for what we see and what we hear.

How do you capture people's stories and experiences around the smells that they experience?

Individual stories and experiences are built into the process of the smell walk; at the end of each section participants discuss their findings and share their individual and shared olfactory histories. At the end of the walk and visualisation, these stories are retold through oral olfactory narratives prompted by visuals. These narratives combine the immediate

past experience with various points in collective and individual memory. One of the Amsterdam smells is named as 'coffee with friends', it's not only 'coffee', it is especially 'to come together with friends' that reflects an intimacy and poignancy. In naming the smells in such a way, my research reveals individual and collective memories, rather than assessing our ability to identify odours. And in the process we come to understand the city in a unique and nuanced way; it's an opportunity to pause, to reflect, to understand places or routines and rhythms that are incredibly familiar but unremarked.

How do you choose how to visualise the collected smells?

When I am creating a smell map I transcribe the smell walkers' smell notes into a database. I also note the weather conditions; wind speed, wind direction, precipitation and temperature (all of which has a bearing on understanding and communicating the smellscape). A dotted pattern for smell dispersal for example, came about when I was researching in Glasgow. There is a particular Glaswegian phenomenon called 'dreich', which is something between fog and rain. It's something you would notice when you walk through it; it hangs rather than falls and feels as if it is harbouring smells. This inspired me to use dots as the symbol to denote smell in a damp or humid atmosphere whereas smells in a windy environment are depicted with a customised isoline symbol.

What kind of purposes do your maps serve, intended or otherwise?

That's always an interesting question and I struggle with where to situate the maps because, for me, they are far more about the research than they are about the outcome. The outcome happens to be aesthetically pleasing, and I'm very proud of them, but I see them mainly as a research tool. Of course there are potential applications within architecture and urban design, as a way to be considerate of all senses while designing and planning and as a record of olfactory heritage. Ultimately, they are provocations and a call to action that says, 'please go out and sniff, smell and explore for yourself'.

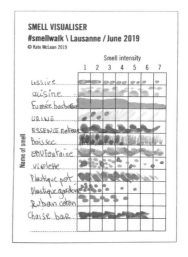

Above: Smell visualiser cards. (Carte des Odeurs). Lausanne, Switzerland. 2019.

Below: Participants of a smellwalk, smell catching and smell hunting in Lausanne, Switzerland. 2019.

Project feature

Singapore prefers not to smell, instead it scents.

Scentscape 06. 2015 — Singapore

The city's warm outdoor streets are redolent with ubiquitous frangipani and jasmine. Whereas interior public spaces tend to be olfactorily-curated to the extent that a local (albeit pungent) fruit, the durian, is forbidden. Commercial environments are frequently scented and carefully designed to demarcate brands in a shopping space.

Sometimes it is hard to imagine the possibility of any perceptible presence of everyday urban smells. Singapore is an island city state with a diversity of cultures, a preoccupation with food and a groundhog day equatorial climate. On what would its 'citizen sensors' remark through scent walking the city?

Eight neighbourhoods were picked by locals as a representative sample of the multicultural aspect of the city. Walks took place in Katong, Kampong Glam, Chinatown, Sentosa, East Coast Parkway, Gardens by the Bay, Little India, Orchard Road and Toa Payoh neighbourhoods. Concentric rings of dots represent an averaged

intensity rating and the number repeats of the rings represent scent duration. The colour scheme was taken from participant choices for each of the neighbourhoods. For each walk the most commonly mentioned scent was selected to represent the neighbourhood. The smellwalk, crowd-sourced data were then checked in each of the remaining neighbourhoods to determine whether or not the scent was also perceived, and only if it did was it added to the map. This process reveals neighbourhoods that counter the commonly-perceived smell; Orchard Road is a notable counter-olfactory zone. Visualisation reveals the olfactory vibrancy of Kampong Glam and Little India over the lightness of the Gardens by the Bay. The rings of scent droplets float across a page, entangling and layering upon each other forming a pressed thread 'felt' of smell. The scentscape of Singapore lingers as tiny droplets encapsulated in the warm humid air.

Kate McLean works at the intersection of human-perceived smellscapes, cartography and the communication of 'eye-invisible' sensed data. She leads international public smellwalks and translates the resulting data using digital design, watercolour, animation, scent diffusion and sculpture into smellscape mappings. She leads the BA Graphic Design programme at Canterbury Christ Church University and also supervises Masters by Research students interested in how they can deploy design to research and communicate a range of social issues from dyslexia in HE to tattoo culture. Visit www.sensorymapping.com to learn more.

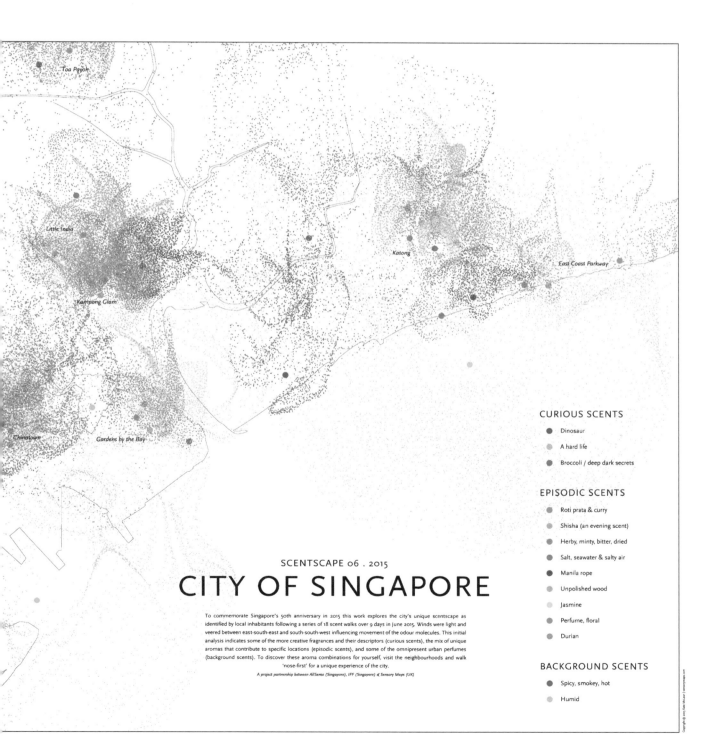

SCENTSCAPE 06 . 2015

CITY OF SINGAPORE

To commemorate Singapore's 50th anniversary in 2015 this work explores the city's unique scentscape as identified by local inhabitants following a series of 18 scent walks over 9 days in June 2015. Winds were light and veered between east-south-east and south-south-west influencing movement of the odour molecules. This initial analysis indicates some of the more creative fragrances and their descriptors (curious scents), the mix of unique aromas that contribute to specific locations (episodic scents), and some of the omnipresent urban perfumes (background scents). To discover these aroma combinations for yourself, visit the neighbourhoods and walk 'nose-first' for a unique experience of the city.

A project partnership between AllSense (Singapore), IFF (Singapore) & Sensory Maps (UK)

CURIOUS SCENTS

- Dinosaur
- A hard life
- Broccoli / deep dark secrets

EPISODIC SCENTS

- Roti prata & curry
- Shisha (an evening scent)
- Herby, minty, bitter, dried
- Salt, seawater & salty air
- Manila rope
- Unpolished wood
- Jasmine
- Perfume, floral
- Durian

BACKGROUND SCENTS

- Spicy, smokey, hot
- Humid

Case study

Internet of Elephants

Visualising animal migration patterns and behavior through data driven maps and animations

By Zeynep Yavuz (CLEVER°FRANKE)

From user journeys to animal journeys
In an increasingly connected world, it is still surprising that we as humans have very little connection to wildlife. Many companies know how people move around cities, how they commute, or which routes they pick for their holidays. By collecting data on movement, it is possible to offer services that make mobility more accessible, efficient, and safe. But animals also move from place to place, and they too need safer routes to complete their journeys. As they encounter several man-made obstacles that sometimes endanger their lives, the need to provide safer animal journeys

becomes more urgent.

Internet of Elephants is a social enterprise based in Kenya and the United States. They are a collaboration of technologists, conservationists, educators, game designers, and strategists working together towards creating a stronger connection between people and wild animals.

They approached us to tell a story based on data to protect the wildlife in Eastern Africa and their habitats. Our solution was to create a short, data-based documentary that maps the individual journey of animals, which we then turned into a series of short

animations. The documentary follows three wild animals: elephant, lions and wildebeest, in order to tell their stories through data collected from their GPS collars. We reveal their incredible migration patterns and the unfortunate man-made obstacles they face in their quest for survival.

We set out by determining three main goals for this project:
• Explain the animal behavior through captivating animation;
• Show the high quality of GPS-collar data gathered by conservationists;
• Drive awareness of human influence on wildlife habitats.

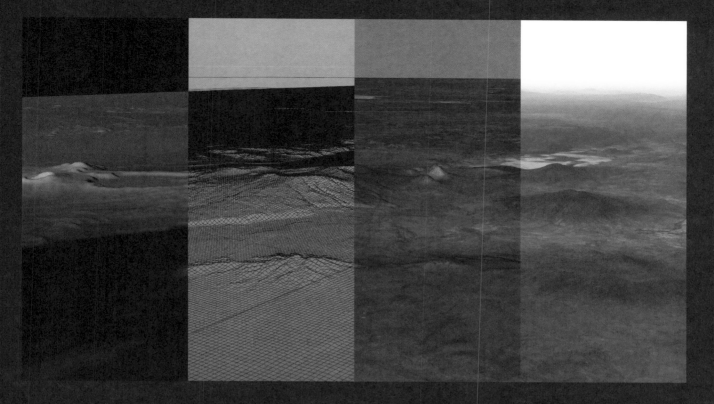

Recreating African landscapes in 3D

When quantitative and qualitative data join forces

World Elephant Center, Gnu Landscapes and Savannah Tracking provided us with data files from each animal containing GPS collar data, with data points referencing movement at regular intervals. Collecting data is an essential part of such a project. However, data should be seen as any other type of content; without putting it into context, there is not much to tell or show.

GPS tracking data can also pose more complexities than what people might expect, especially when it comes to animal movement. When looking at a person's tracking data in a city, it is easier to draw conclusions based on the places that the person visits or the vehicles s/he used. But it becomes extra challenging to make sense of data when looking at the wilderness and how an animal moves around spaces unfamiliar to non-specialists.

For this reason, after analysing the GPS-data from three different groups of animals, we asked a team of conservationists to offer their expertise and provide us with a contextual understanding of their journeys and explanations for abnormal patterns. The interviews we had with the conservation team helped us understand why certain animals choose certain routes. For example, when we looked at the elephant data that was gathered over five months, we saw that they mostly stay around the same area near a river. However, mapping the data revealed their quick forays into human settlements. Conservationists informed us that elephants make these journeys in order to reach Acacia trees and salt pans that provide essential nutrients in their diets.

Once we had removed inconsistencies and interpolated missing references, we processed the data in Python to generate images, graphs and videos of the animal journeys. These formed the basis of the animations, and with the addition of maps and researcher context, completed the stories.

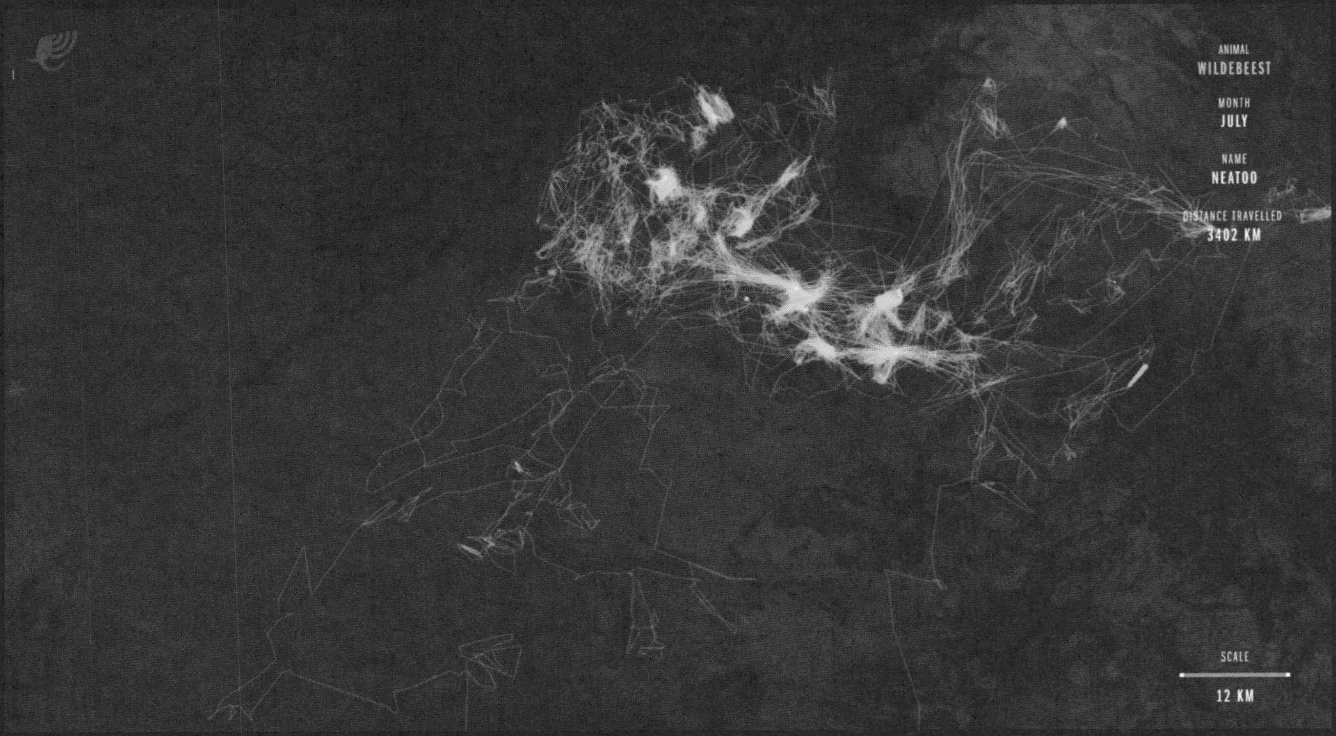

ANIMAL
WILDEBEEST

MONTH
JULY

NAME
NEATOO

DISTANCE TRAVELLED
3402 KM

SCALE

12 KM

Top: The wildebeest; Neatoo: We accompany Neatoo on her journey during the great migration. Mysteriously, Neatoo leaves her herd and joins millions of other wildebeest to graze on the fresh pastures in the Serengeti. The following year, she rejoins her herd back in the north. Her journey shows us the value of maintaining continuity across borders to preserve the complex and wondrous patterns of rain, grass and wildebeest.

Opposite top: Manyara the elephant: The story of Manyara follows a 26-year-old elephant living on Manyara Ranch, a privately owned, protected area in Tanzania. Her tracking data tells us that she regularly makes a risky crossing over a highway to reach a salt pan and satisfy her craving for sodium.

Opposite right: A tale of two lionesses: Sisters Fleur and Valentine are two lionesses living in Soysambu Conservancy, separated when a new fence is erected and divides their territory. Her data illustrates the confrontation between the natural world and human obstructions.

ANIMAL
ELEPHANT

NAME
MANYARA

DISTANCE TRAVELLED
695 KM

MONTH
MARCH - JULY

T17 HIGHWAY

SCALE

3 KM

ANIMAL
LION

NAMES
FLEUR & VALENTINE

MONTH
JUNE

ELECTRIC FENCE

SCALE

4 KM

Bringing the data to life through animated story-telling

To make it a compelling story that our client could use across different platforms, we focused on three different animals for our short documentaries. We began with outlining their stories, sketching storyboards, and determining the look and feel of the animations. With the aid of height maps and satellite imagery, we recreated the African landscapes in 3D onto which we plotted the data.

The final animations follow the animals across the landscapes, highlighting their chosen routes and illustrating the choices behind their behavior.

The power of a multi-disciplinary approach

Data is the main ingredient in most of our projects. It allows us to zoom in and out of stories, reveal valuable insights and turn challenges into actionable solutions for a wide range of audiences.

In this project, thanks to the GPS data that we received, we could track patterns of animal movement and understand abnormal journeys with the help of other data sources. Collecting and mapping this type of data over time and unpacking noticeable divergence helps make it more usable. Highlighting how an elephant herd faces dangers while crossing a highway, or how a lion is blocked by an electric fence and nearly dies, proves that zooming into these patterns helps us create insights upon which specialists can take action.

Data also creates opportunities for us to bring different stakeholders together to tell a holistic story. Our approach to GPS data analysis is different from that of the conservation team; different but complementary. By collaborating with experts in different fields, we can fill knowledge gaps and enrich the overall story by adding important details that make the outcome more complete.

The project we did for Internet of Elephants exemplifies how mapping, data and design can form a powerful, multidisciplinary approach and turn complex patterns into actionable, awareness-raising insights.

Full documentary:
https://vimeo.com/194663029
Project case study description:
https://www.cleverfranke.com/work/
internet-of-elephants

Zeynep Yavuz is Project & PR Assistant at CLEVER°FRANKE. She has an MA in Media Studies Research from the University of Amsterdam.

CLEVER°FRANKE is a design agency focused on data visualization. They create innovative design solutions for data driven clients inspired by their brand values. Their mission is to solve the most complex of challenges, create impact through relevant solutions, to challenge perceptions and inspire change by venturing into the uncharted.

Zooming in and out of complexity

Combining mapping with other methods to present multiple points of view

By Shay Raviv, Dorota Gazy (STBY), and Megan Anderson (STBY)

At STBY, we rarely use system maps in isolation during our research process. If a system map is a deliverable, it is often accompanied by other maps and forms of narrative and visual content like design documentaries, user profiles, and documented interviews. We know the value of system maps in summarising, consolidating and visually communicating complex ecosystems and relationships. But in simplifying and zooming out, we often lose a lot of rich stories, nuance and perspective. We realise that our research deliverables also have different audiences and serve a range of needs in innovation projects. Whereas a system map might be fit for a multi-stakeholder strategy meeting, a more granular user-journey or design documentary might be more valuable for a design team.

Different ways of knowing

Various artefacts can offer different points of view of the area of inquiry. And various points of view are important in understanding and communicating the system in its entirety: from a macro, 'birds eye view', down to a more granular, personal or 'micro' perspective. These perspectives, when presented side by side, can often be complementary and mutually reinforcing.

Recently we have been experimenting with striking a balance between perspectives and scales, and creating more interactive ways of experiencing the systems that we study. On Google Maps we can zoom in and out, and even switch to street-view perspective. How could we recreate a similar experience in a physical space without relying on screens?

For Dutch Design Week 2019 we experimented with the idea of zooming in and out of a complex system in a physical space. As part of the 'GEO—DESIGN:

Junk' exhibition, the installation 'Chiefs of Waste' presented a global investigation, delving into the ever-changing worlds of waste pickers in Mexico City and Bangalore to uncover the networks, actors and structures that span the blurry lines between formal and informal (waste) systems.

Zooming out: System maps highlight the blurry lines between formal and informal waste systems

Waste-pickers perform between 50 and 100 percent of waste collection in most cities in developing countries, according to the United Nations Human Settlements Programme (UN-Habitat). This informal way of waste management fills the gap where official systems are failing, and provides a livelihood for millions of people.

There are an estimated 15 million waste pickers currently operating around the world. Traditionally seen as tokens of the informal economy and often stigmatised, over the past ten years they have begun to organise themselves, seeking recognition, protection and workers' rights. However, there are downsides to becoming a more regulated industry.

The system map we created, printed on a three metre long woven plastic sheet, presented the formal and informal actors in the local waste management economies and the relationships between them. As a guiding logic for our system map we chose the question: who is

THE WASTE PICK

MEXICO CITY   BANGALORE

Funded

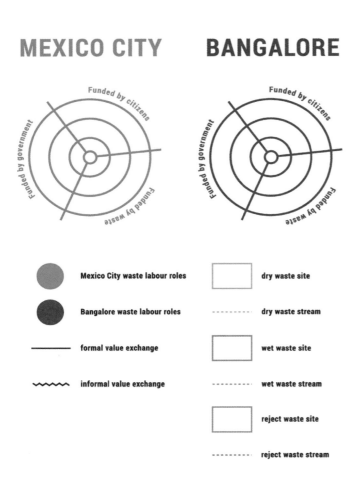

Mexico City's waste labour ecosyste

earning money from waste? This led us to a circular map divided in three sections: government, industry and citizens. This model demonstrates the importance of the informal actors in these two contexts and the nature of these economies, where the lines between the formal and informal blend.

Zooming in: Objects and photography complement the map and make the systems more tangible and human

The system maps that we created proved to be a really effective way of helping people quickly and easily grasp the complexity of the system in which waste pickers operate in Bangalore and Mexico City, respectively. On their own, however, they fail to provide the nuanced, personal

stories of the crucial people, objects and organisations that make up these systems. We wanted viewers to see both the forest and the trees.

To accommodate both perspectives, we sought to 'zoom in' on elements of the system map by collecting, photographing and 'narrating' artefacts found or referenced in our fieldwork. Local researchers from Studio José de la O (Mexico) and Quicksand (India) gathered artefacts used by waste pickers and the stories of the people who use them. We chose this approach for two main reasons. First, as we worked towards an exhibition, we wanted to have tangible research data- not just posters on a wall. We wanted to show that we did not just sit at our desks and map the system purely

OSYSTEM

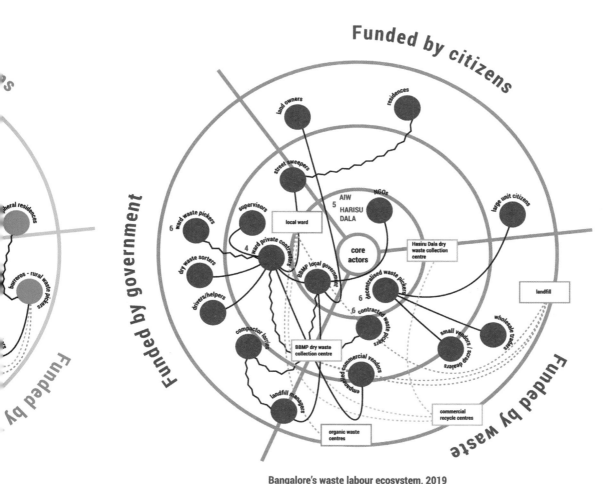

Bangalore's waste labour ecosystem, 2019

through desk research, but went into communities and gained perspectives from multiple sources. While we would have liked to include interview footage and photography, we quickly discovered the sensitivity of the topic, especially in Mexico, where waste pickers are often entangled with the local mafia networks. Gathering personal stories around artefacts that we could showcase proved to be an effective approach.

As gateways to a deeper understanding of wider systems, the artefacts we collected, and the stories to accompany them, were then combined to create portraits of previously elusive organisational work. In doing so, we sought to present the real stories of waste pickers and their struggle to be accepted as important actors in the complex waste economy.

CHIEFS OF WASTE is an installation developed by Dorota Gazy & Shay Raviv in collaboration with STBY (The Netherlands), Studio José de la O (Mexico) and Quicksand (India).

The installation was part of the exhibition GEO—DESIGN: JUNK (All That Is Solid Melts into Trash). A collaboration between Design Academy Eindhoven, Van Abbemuseum and Eindhoven inner city, with the support of BIZ Eindhoven.

DESIGN RESEARCH, MEXICO CITY
Studio José de la O: José de la O, Andrea Michael De la Peña

DESIGN RESEARCH, BANGALORE
Quicksand: Babitha George, Pollyanna Moss, Vinodh Kumar

DESIGN RESEARCH SUPPORT
STBY: Bas Raijmakers, Geke van Dijk, Megan Anderson, Femke Kocken, Nina Stegeman

PHOTOGRAPHY
Studio Pim Top

GRAPHIC DESIGN SUPPORT
DUO44: Michèle Degen & Julia Schäfer

Dorota Gazy is a design researcher at STBY. She is a graduate of Design Academy Eindhoven. Prior to the Design Academy she completed a Bachelor and Master degree Art History at the University of Amsterdam and VU University Amsterdam. As a researcher she seeks hidden patterns and moments where we take things for granted in order to design concepts that raise questions and trigger action.

Shay Raviv is a social designer, project initiator, and design researcher based in The Netherlands. She is a graduate of Design Academy Eindhoven, department Man & Leisure. Raviv works on different projects where culture, design, and creativity are seen as a means to bridge societal gaps. She brings people to the center of a creative process and helps different organisations to better understand the people and context in which they are innovating.

Mapping the tentacular

A reflection on climate futures created by Superflux

By Bas Raijmakers (STBY)

How far can we go in our explorations of what maps could express and how they do so? Several articles in this publication point out the need for pushing the boundaries of our understanding of maps. For instance, by questioning maps as neutral expressions of knowledge. Similarly we should question the assumption that 'clean maps' suggest neutrality and more 'painterly maps' suggest subjectivity. These examples urge us to know and express the origins and intentions of maps when we make them, because they can be instruments to exert control or power.

Maps can sometimes skew our thinking instead of clarifying it. In particular when we use maps to understand wicked problems, as we often attempt in design, the propensity exists to simplify complexities to a level where we can regain overview and control. This is all very understandable in our quest for 'solutions', but is that what we really need if we actually aspire to shift and change the systems that created these wicked problems to begin with?

The climate emergency that we are living in today illustrates this well. When reading the United Nations IPCC reports[1], one is confronted with a multitude of maps based on scientific knowledge. The visuals in these reports push the boundaries of how much data can be conveyed per square inch, and do a great job in translating numbers into insights while remaining neutral and objective in a scientific sense too. But they fail in conveying the experiences of people and other species on this planet today. And even more, they fail in letting us experience the climate futures that these reports sketch through scientific modelling, for instance of rising sea levels, heavy rainfall, severe droughts and soaring summer temperatures.

Next to the IPCC maps, we may also need entirely different maps, as Anab Jain from Superflux states, suggesting additional ways of working: "Modernism's methodologies of mapping, designing, planning, for controlling and changing deeply complex systems may not be the answer to the challenges we face. Maybe we need to go underground — working in networked, symbiotic companionships, like mycelial arrangements, to generate infinite micro-revolutions."[2]

Superflux, the studio Anab Jain leads together with Jon Ardern, is experimenting with these alternatives in their project Mitigation of Shock[3], thus far shown in two versions in Barcelona and Singapore. Mitigation of Shock (MOS) presents itself in the Barcelona exhibition as a London apartment in 2050. This apartment exists in a climate future where food insecurity and social unrest are omnipresent. But instead of scaring visitors who are coming to the apartment, Superflux aims to help people to prepare for such futures by sharing "methods and tools for not only surviving but also thriving there." In that sense we can see the project and the apartment as a map that helps us to navigate the uncertain futures that lay ahead of us.

"All at once somewhat alien, yet strangely familiar, the space gives a rich experiential insight into some of the challenges we could all soon face, and the tactics and strategies we might employ to mitigate and overcome them."[3]

Superflux developed their tools and methods by actually living some of the possible 2050 climate futures and building the necessary infrastructure to make the apartment function in 2050, as a food production facility for instance. MOS is not a conceptual artwork, but a functioning apartment for people to live in. It offers others guidance to replicate and experiment themselves via the Instructables website[4]. Scientific knowledge is one foundation for MOS, to grow the food for instance, using Arduinos to measure and control the environment. MOS also builds on the scientific maps of the IPCC and other climate scientists, but it is as much rooted in the subjective, painterly, experiential and participatory maps mentioned previously because it is an apartment that tells a story about daily life in 2050, including all the usual messy parts of our daily lives.

In the words of Superflux: "Mitigation of Shock is not a prediction, nor a render. (...) [It is] a familiar space to confront our fears and find concrete ways to mitigate the shock of climate change. This space is an invitation for others to enter, to make climate change tangible for those fortunate enough to currently be unaffected by it."[3]

"The philosophical construct of considering 'life as precarious' foregrounds both life and death. It focuses on how human existence is deeply interdependent with other life and therefore necessitates the need for 'care of others', the need for 'being vulnerable to others' and the need to put 'unpredictable encounters at the centre of things'."[2]

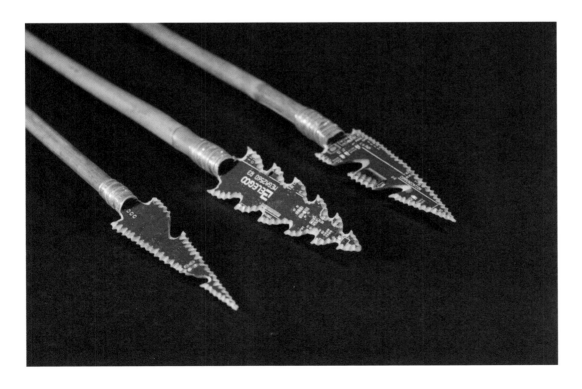

"By seeing the self not as an individual hero, but as one among many — human and non-human — a new kind of tentacular, multi-kind, multi-species politics of care might emerge."2

MOS takes the map from its traditional 2D shape, into an experimental and experiential 4D spacetime. This is necessary for the exploration of what design today still calls wicked problems, but may soon be called 'precarious assemblages' in line with what Superflux suggests2, once we finally understand that 'just' solutions are not the point. MOS helps designers and audiences to navigate beyond problem-solution thinking, towards embracing a more modest role for humans as just one species among many. Humans as a species aim to thrive in ever changing circumstances and situations rather than merely survive, similar to many other species.

The idea of 'assemblage', as a useful addition to 'system', is a part of a new language that Superflux is developing for our uncertain times. In doing so they are standing on the shoulders of other multi-species thinkers and climate philosophers like Donna Haraway5, Bruno Latour6 and others. Writing about why they created MOS, Superflux says: "Over the course of the project, we realised how important it was to explore our deeply entangled relationships with other species and non-human entities. To explore what it would mean to design not simply "tools" that do our bidding, but to design with a more-than-human approach; to design as co-inhabitants of the same complex, ecological system in which humans and non-human species co-exist. A reminder that we don't exist in

"Innovation is a tricky one, unfortunately, co-opted by the association-of-move-fast-and-break-things as (infinite) growth, addition and mutation. Innovation fixates on new; different; change. On the other hand, 'resurgence' (renewing, restoring, regenerating) focuses less on endless growth and more on cyclical forms of nurturing, growing, dying and renewing."[2]

isolation. We never have. But now we are entering a time where we can no longer live in the illusion of isolation, we can either embrace this new understanding and work with its implications or face the hubris of our inaction."[4]

As designers we always want to understand and then take action, or understand through taking action. Maps of many kinds have always played an important role in this approach. Superflux advocates action too, but not in the sense of taking control. They suggest tools for understanding and navigating that are quite different from the neutral, objective maps that are traditionally used to express authority and exert power. Mitigation of Shock is such a 'tool' that may not be immediately apparent as a map to everyone, but definitely offers directions for uncertain travellers in precarious times. By way of assemblage, it maps and provides insight into interdependent relationships between people, other species and technologies.

"Rather than consider a singular
endpoint such as extinction, could
we instead explore the possibility of
life without stability, to begin with,
and see where we arrive?"[2]

Bas Raijmakers is co-founder and Creative Director of STBY in London and
Amsterdam, working for clients in the public sector and industry. Bas has a
background in cultural studies, the early internet industry and interaction
design. His main passion is to bring the people for whom we design into design
and innovation processes, using visual storytelling. He holds a PhD in Design
Interactions from the Royal College of Art, in London. Bas co-founded the Reach
Network for global human centred design and research that STBY is part of.

1 IPCC (Intergovernmental Panel on Climate
Change), "Special Report on Global Warming
of 1.5 °C", accessed 02 August 2020, https://
www.ipcc.ch/sr15/

2 Superflux, "Mitigation of Shock", accessed
02 August 2020, https://www.instructables.
com/id/Mitigation-of-Shock/

3 Superflux, "Calling for a more-than-human
politics", published 23 March 2020, https://
superflux.in/index.php/calling-for-a-more-
than-human-politics/#

4 Superflux, Mitigation of Shock, accessed 02
August 2020, https://superflux.in/index.php/
work/mitigation-of-shock/#

5 Donna Haraway, Staying with the Trouble,
(Duke University Press Books, 2016)

6 Bruno Latour, Facing Gaia: Eight Lectures on
the New Climatic Regime, trans. Cathy Porter
(Polity Press: 2017)

STBY in conversation with Cat Drew (Design Council) and Stephen Bennett (Policy Lab)

Speculative mapping in policymaking

Though they have both spent considerable lengths of time working for various UK government departments, Cat Drew and Stephen Bennett are not your stereotypical policymakers. With backgrounds in design, art and policymaking, the two have shown the power of the polymath in enabling a more creative and participatory form of governance. They are both also huge fans of maps, with impressive collections of mapping projects. We were lucky enough to get them both on a call to chat about mapping in the context of policy making, with a focus on speculative mapping in particular. This is a condensed version of our conversation.

You both seem really into maps. What's with the obsession?

Cat: My grandparents had a boat and every summer we used to sail down the south coast of England and then over to France and back. I just have a really early memory of plotting the course with my granddad, with the sextant and his charts. My job as a five year old would be to make sure we were staying on course, which obviously was nonsense. Most of the time I'd fall asleep halfway through, so I wasn't very good! But there's something kind of deeply personal about discovering where you are going, and also getting lost. It's my way of making sense of the world.

Stephen: I just spent ages in my childhood colouring and tracing maps. My dad was a town planner and he would save and bring back loads of scrap paper for us to use that had been printed on one side with maps. This gave me an early appreciation for the amazing aesthetic of maps. I love really old school maps; when they didn't have much color print they had to be so imaginative with how they distinguished different areas with dots, lines and patterns. With many maps, it's like you're looking at an abstract piece of art.

Why is mapping so relevant to policy making? How does it add value to the process?

Cat: I think there's something really interesting about the map because of its non-linear description of the world, which I think is missing in usual policymaking. When I started policymaking, the way that you would create meaning and understanding would be to sit around a table with lots of people all with their individual documents sharing thoughts one by one. And the way that you would create a policy would be someone would write a document, you'd send it around and people would track changes to it, with the most senior person having the final say.

One of the first maps that Stephen and I created together was an ageing policy map for the Government Office for Science. We basically mapped out all the different policies that affected ageing across government. We designed it nicely, printed a massive version, and got policymakers to walk across it to follow how their policies had consequences for other departments. It was a collective understanding of a situation rather than an individualistic one. Put simply, maps allow policymakers to see themselves as part of a bigger picture.

There's also something about imagination; speculative maps in particular allow you to think outside of the current paradigm. Mapping also enables access to different types of intelligence. You can layer all sorts of data — quantitative and more sensory — onto maps and they can therefore be good translators and sensemaking tools across the vast communities that policies affect. Maps are really accessible too as they provide a basic shared understanding. Finding different ways that people can contribute their thoughts and ideas is really, really important in policymaking. Maps provide a good way of getting people to feel confident in being able to contribute.

Stephen: I completely agree. Maps are a lot less confrontational and intimidating than other things like lengthy policy documents. It's not just two people sitting opposite arguing about text on a page. With maps you can point to things, move things around and draw things together.

There are also so many different ways we learn and communicate. The policymaking world has thus far relied a lot on the verbal and written. Cat and I, and others at the Policy Lab have tried to bring in more visual and kinesthetic ways of understanding and communicating, and maps play a major role in this. It's not just about the diversity of thinking, but it's about diversity of stimulants as well.

What is speculative mapping all about? And what role can it play in policymaking?

Cat: For me, speculative mapping opens up the space. It doesn't necessarily need to come up with a solution. It's not about problem finding. But by opening up the space in an abductive way, you create more license for other people to come up with their own ideas and solutions. We need to get away from this commercial idea that design has to solve problems. What we need is a distributed shift in thinking across lots and lots of different people. We need ways to bring together signals of the future.

But for me what's still an open and interesting question — and this is something we experimented with in the Forest of the Future project — is where do you start with speculative mapping? Do you start with speculative maps as provocations which people then can respond to? Or do you start with an open way of getting people to imagine the future? I'm very interested in how design can create the space for people to be able to access a very different type of consciousness.

Stephen: Speculative mapping is really about provoking conversations about the past, present and future. And the spaces in which we do this are really important too. It's about creating intriguing spaces and prompts where people feel invited and curious about the world around them. But the trick is to not just have them be passive recipients of these provocations. There should be moments where you bring people together and say, 'How do you feel about this? What do you like about this? What do you not like about it? How would you do it if you were to do it and why?'

More broadly, interactive and speculative mapping in particular are relevant in the context of a general disengagement with politics and disillusionment with big data, rational modelling and planning approaches. There's a growing feeling of a loss of control and agency. If you can make a map and then actually allow people to experience and interact with that map, it suddenly starts making the data something that you can smell, taste, feel, discover and change. And I think that's quite an important process: bringing data and actually turning it into something that people can understand, relate to and have a conversation about.

Project feature

Forest of the Future

Following in the footsteps of William Morris' seminal utopian science fiction novel 'News From Nowhere' (1890), Liv Bargman, SRG Bennett, Cat Drew and Phoebe Ridgway created speculations and writings about the future of Waltham Forest. The artworks were exhibited in 'Forest of the Future?' at the Pictorem Gallery in Walthamstow in May to coincide with Waltham Forest's reign as London Borough of Culture 2019.

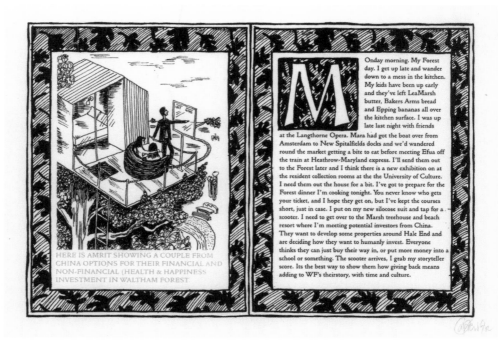

As a cross-disciplinary collective, we applied the emerging discipline of speculative design to the local context of Waltham Forest. Speculative design is the practice of creating visions of a future world: some positive, some less so. The aim is to use these speculations to help decision-makers — politicians, citizens, consumers, voters, businesses — think about what a better future can look like, and how to achieve it. The resulting works are based on local history, trend analysis and technology forecasts. They are fantastical imaginations of what the streets of Waltham Forest could look like. They are sometimes utopian, sometimes dystopian — often oscillating between the two — and always provocative, reflecting this amazing but fraught time for many communities. Growth, regeneration, opportunity, knife crime, gentrification, technology, immigration, populism, stress, dreams and hope — there is so much change, so much up

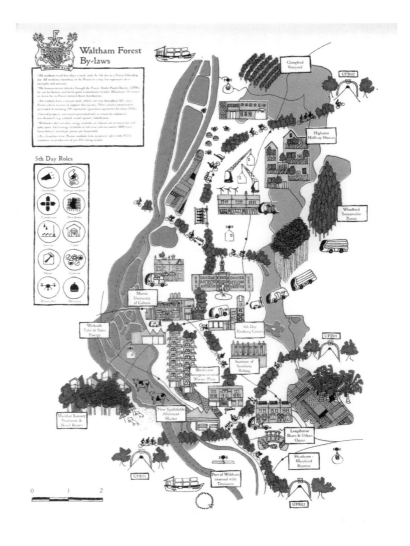

Opposite: A Green Corridor (2019), Liv Bargman, Giclée Print edition of 10, 40 x 26cm

Top: Give & Invest (2019), Cat Drew, Screen Print edition of 12, 21 x 30cm

Right: Waltham Forest By-laws (2019), Cat Drew, Mixed media hand coloured screen print edition of 15, 35 x 50cm

for grabs. Yet the chance of being isolated and disempowered remains stark.

One of the motivations behind speculative design is that it is better to talk about the future than not: by speculating more and exploring alternative scenarios, reality becomes something we are more empowered to change. We can't predict the future, but we can think about what we do and don't want; that is democratising in itself. This has additional worth when big data, global finance and geopolitics appear to diminish choice. When you engage with these works, ask yourself the question: what do we want our Waltham Forest to be in the future?

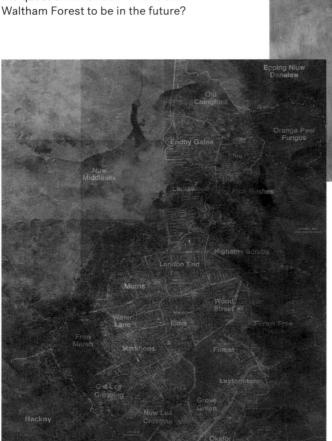

Above: Pools (2019), Phoebe Ridgway, Oil on Board, 45 x 47cm

Left: Forest of the Future? (2019), SRG Bennett, Giclée Print edition of 15, 16 x 20in

Cat Drew is the Chief Design Officer at Design Council where she brings together architecture and the built environment, public sector design and business innovation to support people live healthier, happier and safer lives. Previously, Cat has held leadership positions at FutureGov and Uscreates, was a co-founder of the UK Government's Policy Lab, and combines 10 years of experience in Government with an MA in Graphic Design. She speaks widely about the value of design and co-presents BBC Radio 4 The Fix.

Stephen Bennett is a multimedia artist working in policy-making and science. After studying MA Art and Science at Central St Martins, Stephen focused his practice on the relationship between evidence, emotions and political action. In parallel Stephen is prototyping the application of artistic practices in a UK policy-making context, working part-time for the Cabinet Office's Policy Lab.

Image credits

p. 4
Harry Furniss. (1893). *Lewis Carroll: Sylvie and Bruno Concluded* [Illustration]. https://en.wikisource.org/wiki/Sylvie_and_Bruno_Concluded/The_Man_in_the_Moon#/media/File:Sylvie_and_Bruno_illustration_scan_60.png

p. 11–13
Images © More than Metrics. Used with permission.

p. 15–17
Images © Paper Giant. Used with permission.

p. 19–23
Images recreated from Grimes, J. (2018). *Using a Service Ecosystem to Quickly Grasp Complexity.* https://www.service-design-network.org/community-knowledge/using-a-service-ecosystem-to-quickly-grasp-complexity. Recreated with permission.

p. 24–27
Project sketches by STBY.
Final visuals for Clean Energy Challenge by What Design Can Do https://cleanenergychallenge.whatdesigncando.com/

p. 29–30
Images © STBY

p. 31
Design Council (2019). *Double Diamond* [Illustration]. https://www.designcouncil.org.uk/news-opinion/what-framework-innovation-design-councils-evolved-double-diamond.

p. 32
Drew, C. (2019). *Workshop at the 2019 Service Design Global Conference Toronto* [Photographs].

p. 36
De Wit, F. (1670). *Celestial map* [Map]. https://commons.wikimedia.org/wiki/File:Planisph%C3%A6ri_c%C5%93leste.jpg

Wellcome Collection, & Snow, J. (1854). *Plan Showing the Ascertained Deaths from Cholera* [Photograph]. Wellcome Collection. https://wellcomecollection.org/works/dx4prdbj

p. 37
Vignelli, M. (1974). *New York City Subway Map* [Map]. Museum of Modern Art. https://www.moma.org/collection/works/89299?sov_referrer=artist&artist_id=0&page=2

Hertzs, M., & Tauranac, J. (2019). *The official Hertz-style 2019 subway map* [Map]. https://en.wikipedia.org/wiki/New_York_City_Subway_map#/media/File:Official_New_York_City_Subway_Map_vc.jpg

p. 38
Bhāvaprakāśa. (1800). *A human anatomical figure* [Drawing]. Wellcome Library. https://wellcomecollection.org/works/dfcp3k9d/images?id=amts9ckx

A phrenological chart published in 1859. (1859). [Illustration]. https://commons.wikimedia.org/wiki/File:Phrenology%E2%80%94Numbering_and_Definition_of_the_Organs.png

p. 39
McCallum, D., & Henshaw, G. H. (1855). *Organizational diagram of the New York and Erie Railroad* [Illustration]. https://commons.wikimedia.org/wiki/File:Organizational_diagram_of_the_New_York_and_Erie_Railroad,_1855.jpp.

p. 40
Massachusetts Institute of Technology's Senseable City Lab. (n.d.). *A screenshot of an interactive map produced by MIT's Senseable City Lab visualizing exports of e-waste* [Map]. GPS Tracking Devices Catch Major U.S. Recyclers Exporting Toxic E-Waste. https://theintercept.com/2016/05/10/gps-tracking-devices-catch-major-u-s-recyclers-in-improper-e-waste-exports/

p. 41
Priestly, J. (1769). *A New Chart of History color* [Infographic]. University of Oregon InfoGraphics Lab. https://commons.wikimedia.org/wiki/File:A_New_Chart_of_History_color.jpp.

Minard, C. (1869). *Figurative Chart* [Lithograph]. https://en.wikipedia.org/wiki/File:Minard.png

p. 42
Shark, D. (2009). *Comparison of different types of graphical projection* [Graph]. https://commons.wikimedia.org/wiki/File:Graphical_projection_comparison.png

Reveley, W. (1791). *Plan of Jeremy Bentham's panopticon prison* [Drawing]. https://en.wikipedia.org/wiki/Panopticon#/media/File:Panopticon.jpp.

p. 43
Hermann, F. G. (n.d.). *Bad Schussenried, Kloster Schussenried, Neuer Konventsbau, Bibliothekssaal Deckenfresko, Ausschnitt: Baum des Porphyrius* [Painting]. https://commons.wikimedia.org/wiki/File:Schussenried_Kloster_Bibliothekssaal_Gew%C3%B6lbefresko_Baum_des_Porphyrius.jpp.

Konstable. (2007). *An example of a Semantic Network* [Illustration]. https://commons.wikimedia.org/wiki/File:Semantic_Net_mk.svg

p. 44
Ortelius, A. (1595). *Abraham Ortelius' map of Utopia* [Map]. https://commons.wikimedia.org/wiki/File:Utopia.ortelius.jpp.

p. 45
Kunstmuseum Den Haag (2016). *Stills from Video: Constant New Babylon* [Illustration]. https://vimeo.com/168779709

Howard, E. (1898). *To-morrow: A Peaceful Path to Real Reform* [Diagram]. Swan Sonnenschein & Co., Ltd., London. https://commons.wikimedia.org/wiki/File:Diagram_No.7_(Howard,_Ebenezer,_To-morrow.).jpp.

p. 46
Bonpland, Aimé, Arzt, Naturforscher, Entdeckungsreisender, & Frankreich. (1807). *Ideen zu einer Geographie der Planzen nebst einem Naturgemälde der Tropenländer* [Table]. Zentralbibliothek Zürich. https://commons.wikimedia.org/wiki/File:Zentralbibliothek_Z%C3%BCrich_-_Ideen_zu_einer_Geographie_der_Pflanzen_nebst_einem_Naturgem%C3%A4lde_der_Tropenl%C3%A4nder_-_000012142.jpp.

Weitsch, F. G. (1806). *Alexander von Humboldt und Aimé Bonpland am Fuß des Vulkans Chimborazo* [Painting]. https://commons.wikimedia.org/wiki/File:Humboldt-Bonpland_Chimborazo.jpp.

p. 47
Butterworth, J. (1855). *Coloured mezzotint: Florence Nightingale* [Mezzotint]. Wellcome library. https://wellcomecollection.org/works/f7fap3ah

Nightingale, F. (1858). *Diagram of the causes of mortality in the army in the East* [Diagram]. https://commons.wikimedia.org/wiki/File:Nightingale-mortality.jpp.

p. 50-54
Images © The Berlage. Used with permission.

p. 57
Omplexity. (2020). *Mapping Taiwan's Response to COVID-19* [Illustration]. https://www.omplexity.com/covid19.

p. 60
Magnus, O. (1539). *Carta Marina* [Map]. James Ford Bell Library, University of Minnesota. https://apps.lib.umn.edu/bell/map/OLAUS/indexo.html

Bolton. (1766). *Map of Africa, from Malachy Postlethwayt* [Map]. The Universal Dictionary of Trade and Commerce. https://library.princeton.edu/visual_materials/maps/websites/africa/maps.html

p. 61
Smaply the Blog. (2019). *Snippet of a user journey map* [Illustration]. https://www.smaply.com/blog

1:20,000 Topographic Map Legend. (n.d.). [Photograph]. Flickr. https://www.flickr.com/photos/manitobamaps/2152347521

p. 62
L.J., Moss, O., & Irving, A. (n.d.). *Participatory Mapping with Homeless People* [Illustration]. https://researchportal.northumbria.ac.uk/files/20654545/018_Imaging_Homelessness_in_a_City_of_Care.pdf

p. 63
Sletto, B., & UT-Austin. (n.d.). *Participatory map of Yukpa territory, Toromo, Zulia,*

Venezuela. [Illustration]. Participatory Mapping Practice. https://sites.utexas.edu/participatory-mapping/participatory-mapping-practice/

Growing Up Boulder. (n.d.). *Printed, bilingual child-friendly city map--side 1* [Illustration]. Growing Up Boulder. http://www.growingupboulder.org/printed-child-friendly-city-map.html

p. 64
S, H., Gladeema, N. F., Ahmedin, A., Moreau, M., & Tounkara, K. (n.d.). *Counter Cartographies of Exile* [Illustration]. This Is Not an Atlas. https://notanatlas.org/maps/counter-cartographies-exile/?pdf=1201

Guide by Grassroots Mapping with Balloons and Kites - Public Lab. (n.d.). *Grassroots Mapping with Balloons and Kites* [Illustration]. This Is Not an Atlas. https://notanatlas.org/maps/a-view-from-above/

p. 65
Covarrubias, M. (1940). *Peoples of the Pacific* [Illustration]. https://commons.wikimedia.org/wiki/File:Peoples_of_the_Pacific_(35048886141).jpp.

Dear Hunter. (2019). *The Vast Emptiness* [Map]. Cartopological Landscape Sample Atlas of the Euregio Meuse-Rhine. https://www.yumpu.com/en/document/view/62819709/cartopological-landscape-sample-atlas-of-the-euregio-meuse-rhine-excerpt

p. 68
Rothuizen, J. (n.d.). *The smell of prison* [Illustration]. Temporary Museum. Amsterdam, NL.

Wood, D. (2013). *JACK-O'-LANTERNS* [Illustration]. In Everything Sings: Maps For A Narrative Atlas (2nd Revised and Expanded ed.).

p. 69
Renoir, P. (1877). *Portrait of Jeanne Samary* [Painting]. The Pushkin Museum of Fine Arts, Moscow. https://pushkinmuseum.art/data/

fonds/europe_and_america/j/2001_3000/zh_3405/index.php?lang=en

Ingres, J. (1848). *Portrait of the Baronness James de Rothschild* [Painting]. Art Renewal Center Museum. https://commons.wikimedia.org/wiki/File:Jean_auguste_dominique_ingres_baronne_james_de_rothschild.jpp.

p. 70
Allen, T. & Queen, S. (2015). Debate and deliberation in critical cartography [illustration]. http://visiblelanguage.herokuapp.com/issue/172/article/1192.

p. 72-75
Images © Kate McLean. Used with permission.

p. 76-79
Images © CLEVER°FRANKE. Used with permission.

p. 82-84
Images © STBY

p. 86-90
Images © Superflux. Used with permission.

p. 92
Bargman, L. (2019). *A Green Corridor* [Giclée]. SRG Bennett. https://www.srgbennett.com/forest-of-the-future

p. 93
Drew, C. (2019a). *Give & Invest* [Screen print]. SRG Bennett. https://www.srgbennett.com/forest-of-the-future

Drew, C. (2019b). *Waltham Forest By-laws* [Screen print]. SRG Bennett. https://www.srgbennett.com/forest-of-the-future

p. 94
Ridgway, P. (2019). *Pools* [Painting]. SRG Bennett. https://www.srgbennett.com/forest-of-the-future

Bennett, S. (2019). *Forest of the Future?* [Giclée]. SRG Bennett. https://www.srgbennett.com/forest-of-the-future